Science Fair

j507 8

G17655

Science Projects About Physics in the Home

Robert Gardner

Science Projects

Enslow Publishers, Inc.

40 Industrial Road   PO Box 38
Box 398   Aldershot
Berkeley Heights, NJ 07922   Hants GU12 6BP
USA   UK
http://www.enslow.com

Library of Congress Cataloging-in-Publication Data

Gardner, Robert, 1929–
    Science projects about physics in the home / Robert Gardner.
        p. cm. — (Science projects)
    Includes bibliographical references and index.
    Summary: Presents instructions for physics projects and experiments that can be
done at home and exhibited at science fairs.
    ISBN 0-89490-948-7
    1. Physics—Experiments—Juvenile literature. 2. Science projects—Juvenile
literature. 3. Science—Exhibitions—Juvenile literature. [1. Physics—Experiments.
2. Experiments. 3. Science projects.] I. Title. II. Series: Gardner, Robert, 1929–
Science projects.
QC26.G37   1999
507.8—dc21   98-6822
                                              CIP
                                              AC

Printed in the United States of America

10 9 8 7 6 5 4 3

To Our Readers:
All Internet addresses in this book were active and appropriate when we went to press. Any
comments or suggestions can be sent by e-mail to Comments@enslow.com or to the address
on the back cover.

Illustration Credits: Stefanie Rowland

Cover Illustration: Jerry McCrea (foreground); © Corel Corporation (background).

Contents

*appropriate ideas for science fair project

*appropriate ideas for science fair project

Introduction

This book is filled with projects and experiments that are related to physics, the study of matter and energy. Most of the materials you will need to carry out these activities can be found in your home or school. Several of the experiments may require materials that you can buy in a supermarket, a hobby or toy shop, or a hardware store. You will need someone to help you with a few activities that require more than one pair of hands. It would be best if you work with friends or adults who enjoy experimenting as much as you do. In that way you will both enjoy what you are doing. **If any danger is involved in doing an experiment, it will be clearly stated in the text. In some cases, to avoid any danger to you, you will be asked to work with an adult. Please do so.** We do not want you to take any chances that could lead to an injury.

Like a good scientist, you will find it useful to record your ideas, notes, data, and anything you can conclude from your experiments in a notebook. By so doing, you can keep track of the information you gather and the conclusions you reach. Record keeping will allow you to refer to experiments you have done that may help you in doing other projects in the future.

Today, physicists and chemists assume that matter is made up of atoms and molecules. There is good evidence for believing that atoms and molecules exist, but in this book we will simply assume their existence.

Science Fairs

Most of the projects in this book may be appropriate for a science fair. Those projects are indicated with an asterisk (*). However, judges at such fairs do not reward projects or experiments that are simply copied from a book. For example, using a prism to break white light into the multicolored spectrum of which it is composed would probably not impress judges; however, a series of experiments designed to find out which colors (wavelengths) are absorbed by different pigments would be more likely to receive serious consideration.

Science fair judges tend to reward creative thought and imagination. It is difficult to be creative or imaginative unless you are really interested in your project; consequently, be sure to choose a subject that appeals to you. And before you jump into a project, consider, too, your own talents and the cost of materials you will need.

If you decide to use a project found in this book for a science fair, you should find ways to modify or extend it. This should not be difficult because you will probably discover that as you do these projects, new ideas for experiments will come to mind—experiments that could make excellent science fair projects, particularly because the ideas are your own and are interesting to you.

If you decide to enter a science fair and have never done so before, you should read some of the books listed in the Further Reading section as well as *Science Fair Projects—Planning, Presenting, Succeeding*, which is one of the other books in this series. These books deal specifically with science fairs and will provide plenty of helpful hints and lots of useful information that will enable you to avoid the pitfalls that sometimes plague first-time entrants. You will learn how to prepare appealing reports that include charts and graphs, how to set up and display your work, how to present your project, and how to relate to judges and visitors.

Safety First

Most of the projects included in this book are perfectly safe. However, the following safety rules are well worth reading before you start any project.

1. Do any experiments or projects, whether from this book or of your own design, under the supervision of a science teacher or other knowledgeable adult.

2. Read all instructions carefully before proceeding with a project. If you have questions, check with your supervisor before going any further.

3. Maintain a serious attitude while conducting experiments. Fooling around can be dangerous to you and to others.

4. Wear approved safety goggles when you are working with a flame or doing anything that might cause injury to your eyes.

5. Do not eat or drink while experimenting.

6. Have a first-aid kit nearby while you are experimenting.

7. Do not put your fingers or any object other than properly designed electrical connectors into electrical outlets.

8. Never experiment with household electricity except under the supervision of a knowledgeable adult.

9. Do not touch a lit high-wattage bulb. Lightbulbs produce light, but they also produce heat.

10. Many substances are poisonous. Do not taste them unless instructed to do so.

11. Keep flammable materials such as alcohol away from flames and other sources of heat.

12. If a thermometer breaks, inform your adult supervisor. Do not touch either the mercury or the broken glass with your bare hands.

1

Physics in
Your Living Room

A good scientist can find questions every place he or she looks. The home is no exception. That is why each chapter in this book is about a particular place in or near your home where you can do experiments as you learn more about science. The experiments in this book have a physics "flavor," but they may, at times, spill over into what might be considered other fields of science as well. We begin with experiments you could do in your living room, but feel free to turn the pages to another chapter and start there if you prefer. Or you may want to do some of these living-room experiments in another place. Do not let walls constrain your appetite for experimenting.

1-1*
Where's Your Center—
of Gravity, That Is!

A Ping-Pong Ball's Center of Gravity

This experiment begins in your living room with two observations—one of them surprising—involving a deck of playing cards, two new unsharpened pencils, and a Ping-Pong ball. Cut the deck of cards in half and put the two halves side by side on a table. Place the eraser ends of the two unsharpened pencils close to each other on the cards as shown in Figure 1a. The other ends of the pencils should be about 4 cm (1.5 in) apart on the table. Place the Ping-Pong ball at the center of the two pencils. To no one's surprise, the ball rolls down the pencils to the table.

Now reverse the pencils as shown in Figure 1b. Use the edge of a book or a paperweight to hold the erasers in place on the table. The other ends of the pencils are now on the cards and about 4 cm (1.5 in) apart. Again place the ball at the midpoint of the two pencils. Which way does the ball roll this time? Can you explain why?

The surprising observation you have just made has to do with the ball's center of gravity—the point where all of an object's

Things you will need:
- deck of playing cards
- 2 new unsharpened pencils with erasers
- Ping-Pong ball
- paperweight or book
- flat ruler
- sharpened pencil
- shears
- sheet of cardboard
- straight pin
- thread
- heavy washer
- pillow
- chair
- an adult
- wall
- partner
- full-length mirror (optional)
- pack of cards or chalkboard eraser
- several friends or classmates

9

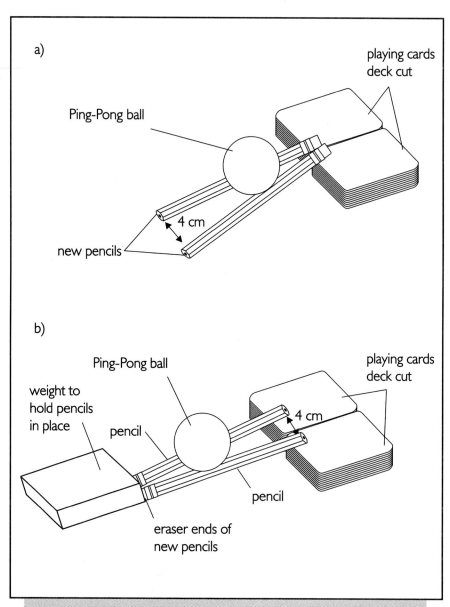

a)

playing cards
deck cut

Ping-Pong ball

new pencils

4 cm

b)

Ping-Pong ball

playing cards
deck cut

weight to
hold pencils
in place

pencil

4 cm

eraser ends of
new pencils

pencil

Figure 1. Which way will the Ping-Pong ball roll in (a)? in (b)? Can you explain what is happening in each case?

weight can be considered to be. This is the point where an object's weight is balanced so that the object has no tendency to rotate one way or the other. It is also the point where you can pick up the object without its turning in any way. In Figure 1b, for the ball's center of gravity, the direction down was toward the cards, toward the open end of the pencils; consequently, the ball rolled that way.

A Ruler's Center of Gravity

The center of gravity (COG) of any object can be found. In the case of a uniform sphere, its COG—as you might guess—is at its center, the point where all its weight can be considered to be. In the case of a ruler, the task is somewhat more difficult. You can balance a flat ruler quite easily by placing your finger under the center of the ruler as shown in Figure 2a. This tells you that the COG lies at the center of the ruler. If you place your finger under the ruler to the right of the center, the ruler rotates counterclockwise and falls off your finger. If you place your finger under the ruler to the left of the center, the ruler rotates clockwise and falls off your finger. Whenever an object's COG lies outside its point of support, it will rotate. To be stable, a body's COG must lie directly under or over a single point of support or between two or three points of support.

Now, using your finger, try to balance the ruler on its long edge (Figure 2b), its end (Figure 2c), and its corner (Figure 2d). As you will find, the higher the center of gravity, the more difficult it is to make the ruler (or anything else) balance. The slightest motion puts the ruler's COG at a position that is not directly above its point of support.

If the ruler has an opening through it near one end, support the ruler at that point on the end of a sharpened pencil (Figure 2e). You will see that the ruler hangs so that its COG lies below its point of support. What happens if you pull the lower end of the ruler in Figure 2e to one side and release it? Where does the COG eventually come to rest?

11

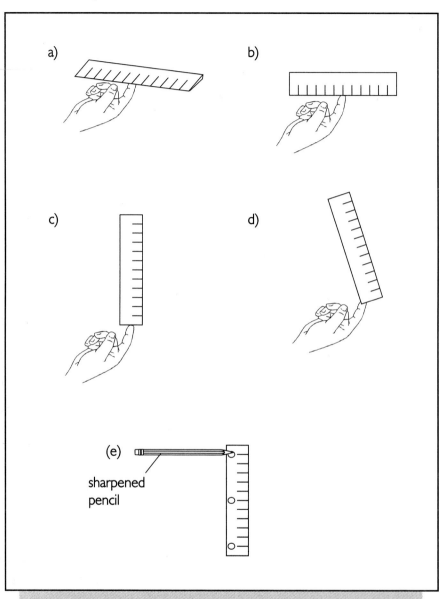

a)

b)

c)

d)

(e)   sharpened pencil

Figure 2. A ruler will balance if the support point is located beneath its COG. That is not always easy to do.

An Irregular Shape's Center of Gravity

Use shears to cut a sheet of cardboard into an irregular shape such as the one shown in Figure 3. To find the COG of such an irregular shape, first make a plumb line. You can make such a line with a straight pin, thread, and a heavy washer as shown in Figure 3. Tie one end of the thread to the pin, the other end to the washer. Use the pin to hang the irregular shape on something such as a bulletin board. The shape should be able to swing freely. Follow the thread with a pencil to make a line on the cardboard. Since the washer at the end of the plumb line is attracted by gravity toward the earth's center, your line will have that direction as well. Hang the shape from a number of different points after turning it a few degrees and mark the thread-line for each position. As you will find, the lines

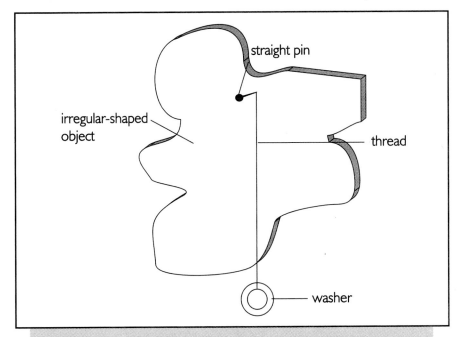

Figure 3. The center of gravity of an object with an irregular shape can be found by using a plumb line. The line is attached to each of several different points of support from which the object is hung free to rotate about its point of support.

all meet (or nearly meet) at one point. This point, which was always below the pin supporting the irregular shape, is its COG.

To test this method for finding an object's COG, take down the cardboard and place the point where the lines meet on your fingertip. Does the shape balance on your finger? If it does, what does that tell you about the point on the cardboard? Can you balance the cardboard at any other point?

Use the technique you have just learned to find the COG for other objects. Can you use this method to find the COG of three-dimensional objects?

Your Own Center of Gravity

You can find the approximate location of your own center of gravity quite easily. Place a pillow on the back of a chair and **ask an adult** to hold the chair while you lie with your lower abdomen on the pillow and your arms at your sides. Your COG probably lies a few inches below your belly button. When you are balanced on the back of the chair (Figure 4), you know your COG lies at a point directly above where your body balances on the chair. Of course, that point is inside your body about halfway from your abdomen to your back.

To see what happens when your COG lies beyond your feet, knees, or other points of support (for people who like to walk on their hands), try these experiments.

Heels Against the Wall

Stand with your heels against a wall. Then try to bend over and touch your toes. To see why you can't touch your toes with your heels against a wall, watch someone else (or yourself in a full-length mirror) as he bends to touch his toes. What happens to the center of the person's body as he lowers his shoulders and arms toward his toes? What happens to the position of that person's COG as he

14

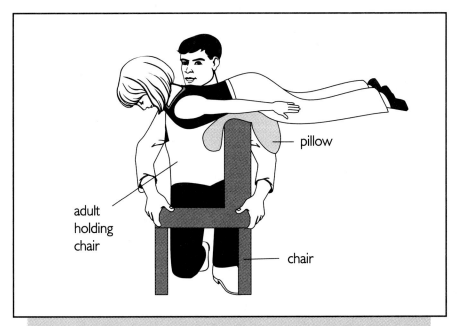

adult
holding
chair

pillow

chair

Figure 4. You can find your own center of gravity quite easily.

bends over? Why must the COG move as it does if the person is to remain on his feet?

Toes Against the Wall

Watch that same person move as he goes from a normal stance to one where he is standing on his toes. How does his body move? Why does it move that way? Try to predict what will happen if you stand with your toes against a wall and then try to stand on your toes. Try it! Was your prediction correct?

Your Nose and Your COG

A fun thing to try at a party or in a science class can help locate a person's COG. Ask someone to get on the floor on her hands and knees. Place a pack of cards or a chalkboard eraser on its end one cubit in front of her knees as shown in Figure 5. (A cubit is the distance from a person's elbow to the fingertips of the outstretched hand.) After

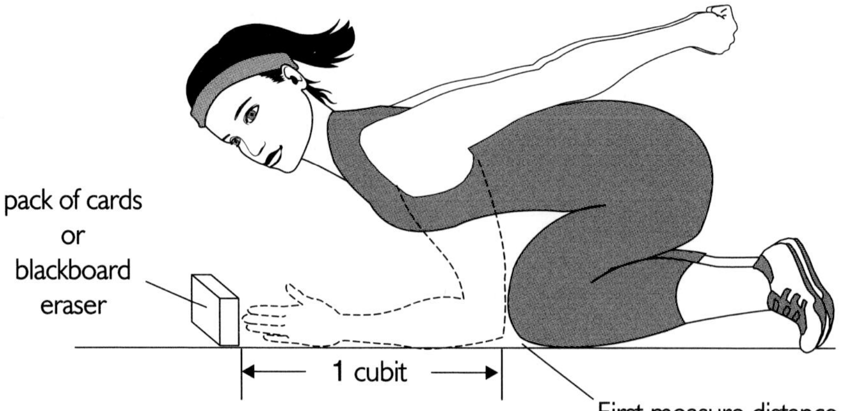
pack of cards
or
blackboard
eraser
1 cubit
First measure distance,
then place both hands
behind back.

Figure 5. How does the location of a person's center of gravity affect that person's ability to knock over a pack of cards or an eraser with his or her nose?

measuring the distance, the person puts both her hands behind her back. Then she tries to tip the pack of cards or eraser over with her nose. Keep your eyes on participants' COG as they attempt to knock over the cards or eraser. How is their COG related to their ability to maintain their balance?

How many people can do this? What does this have to do with a person's COG? Do women and girls seem to be able to do this more easily than men and boys? Does COG seem to be gender-related?

1-2*
"Stopping" a Spinning Fan

Turn on an electric fan. Be sure the fan has a protective screen so there is no danger of your fingers being cut by the fan blades. Notice that you cannot see the blades because they are spinning too fast. Now place the fan in front of a television screen or a computer monitor and turn on the set or monitor in a darkened room. You'll find that you can see the fan blades. They appear to be either stopped or spinning slowly forward or backward.

If the speed of the fan blades can be adjusted, change the speed until the blades appear to be stopped or very nearly so. What happens if you slowly increase the fan's speed? If you decrease the fan's speed?

Things you will need:

- electric fan with a protective screen
- television screen or computer monitor

If you make a strobe, you will need:

- sheet of cardboard
- protractor
- ruler
- pencil
- scissors or shears
- spike
- tape
- stopwatch or watch or clock with a second hand or mode
- partner

If the speed cannot be changed, turn off the fan and watch the blades in front of the screen as they slow down from top speed to zero. You will see the blades appear to stop, rotate slowly forward or backward, stop again, rotate slowly again, and so on, until the blades finally stop.

Although we cannot see it because it happens so fast, a television screen or a computer monitor does not emit light constantly the way an incandescent lightbulb does; instead, the screen or monitor emits light intermittently like a strobe light at intervals, say, 1/50 second apart. (The intervals are not actually 1/50 second. You can try to determine what they really are later.) If the

17

light comes on 50 times per second and the fan is rotating at 50 turns per second, the fan blades will always appear to be at the same place. If the fan makes 100 rotations per second, it will still appear stopped but will make two turns between light flashes. Assuming the fan blades are symmetrical, the fan will also appear to be stopped if it makes 25 or 12.5 turns per second because it will have made half or a quarter of a turn between light flashes.

Suppose, however, that the fan is making 51 turns per second. It will then appear to be turning slowly forward because it will complete slightly more than one turn between light flashes. Similarly, if it is rotating 49 times per second, it will appear to move slowly backward because it makes a little less than one turn between light flashes.

Why do you think the images of a rotating fan seen in front of a television screen or computer monitor have a wavy appearance?

If you have, or can borrow, an adjustable-rate strobe light, you can measure the rotational speeds of a great variety of objects.

If you do not have a strobe light, you can make a hand-operated strobe (stroboscope) as shown in Figure 6. With a partner to operate a stopwatch or watch a clock, you can count the turns you make every 20 seconds when the rotating object appears stopped as viewed through your turning handmade strobe. How can you be sure you are measuring the actual rate of rotation rather than twice, three times, half, or a third of the rate? Hint: What happens if you double the rate at which you turn the strobe?

Exploring on Your Own

How can you use your handmade strobe to determine the actual flash rate (refresh rate) of your television screen or computer monitor?

How can you use a strobe light and any additional equipment you may need to measure the speed of a toy train moving along a straight track?

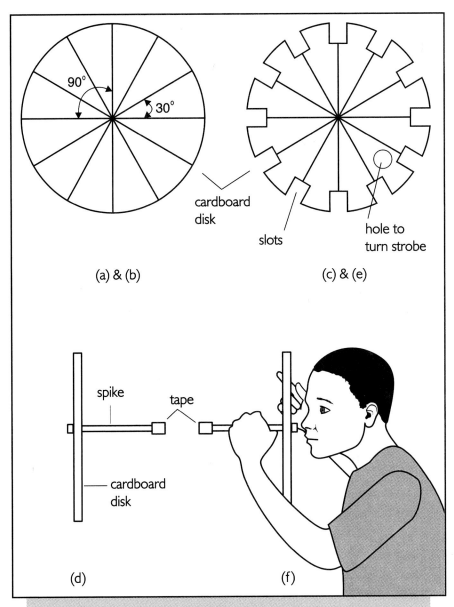

90°

30°

cardboard
disk

slots

hole to
turn strobe

(a) & (b)

(c) & (e)

spike   tape

cardboard
disk

(d)

(f)

Figure 6. To make a handheld strobe: (a) Cut a circle about 30 cm (12 in) in diameter from a sheet of cardboard. (b) Using a protractor, ruler, and pencil, divide the circle into twelve 30-degree pie-shaped pieces. (c) Cut 2-cm x 4-cm (3/4-in x 1 1/2-in) slots at the end of each radius you drew in step 2. (d) Push a spike to serve as a handle through the center of the cardboard disk. Cover the sharp end with tape. (e) Cut a hole 3 cm (1 in) in diameter below and between two slots as shown. You will use the hole to turn the strobe with your finger. (f) Hold the strobe by its handle. Spin it with the index finger of your other hand as you look through the slots in the disk.

How can you use a strobe light and any additional equipment you may need to measure the acceleration (the rate of change of the speed) of a falling object?

Explain why the wheels of cars or wagons seen in motion pictures sometimes appear to be stopped, moving slowly forward, or even backwards.

Use your handmade stroboscope to determine the rate at which the frames in a motion picture are shown.

Sports films are sometimes made in "slow motion" so coaches and players can see their actions more clearly. How are slow motion films made?

1-3*
Persistence of Vision

Even though the images on a television screen, computer monitor, or movie screen are not moving, we see them as moving because of persistence of vision. When an image of an object is formed on the retina of your eye, it does not disappear the moment the object leaves your

Things you will need:

• electric fan

• sheet of cardboard

• scissors

• colored photo or picture

• index card

• thumbtack

• new pencil with eraser

view. The image remains on your retina for about 0.07 second. If a similar but slightly changed image falls on your retina within that time, you see a smooth transition from one image to the next. Because the still images seen on motion picture film and television screens change at intervals of 0.04 second or less, they do not appear as a series of still pictures but rather convey smooth, continuous, natural motion.

There are many ways to demonstrate persistence of vision. One way is to look through a spinning fan. Even though the fan is constantly cutting off part of your view, you see objects on the other side of the fan in their entirety. If you look through the fan when it is stopped, you will be surprised to see how much of your view is blocked by the blades.

Another way to demonstrate persistence of vision is to cut a slot in a sheet of cardboard as shown in Figure 7a. Hold the slot over a picture in bright light. You can see only a small portion of the picture. Now move the cardboard sheet back and forth across the picture as rapidly as you can. Because of persistence of vision, you are able to see the entire picture even though you see only a small part of it at any one moment.

For an object to be seen, it must stay in your view for at least a small fraction of a second in order to form an image on the retina

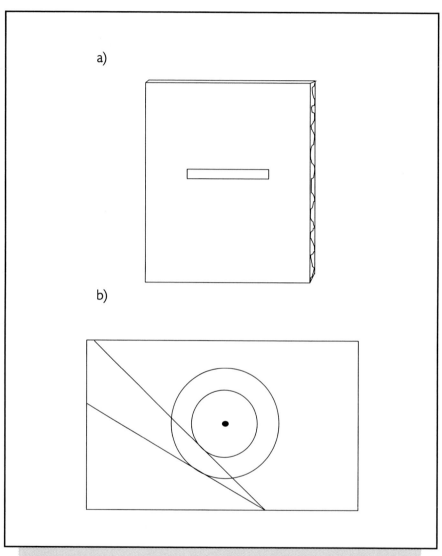

a)

b)

Figure 7. a) A sheet of cardboard with a slot in it will allow you to see an entire picture if it is moved rapidly back and forth across the picture. b) What happens to the straight lines when you spin the card rapidly about its center?

of your eye. To see that this is true, make a card like the one shown in Figure 7b. Push a thumbtack through the center of the card into the eraser of a new pencil. Use your finger to make the card spin rapidly about its center. What happens to the straight lines when the card is spinning?

Exploring on Your Own

Design some demonstrations of your own to illustrate persistence of vision.

2

Physics in Your Bedroom

One nice thing about doing experiments in your own room is that you can do them without a lot of interruptions. However, if you share your room, be sure to give consideration to the person or persons with whom you share it. Don't invade their privacy, but do give them the opportunity to help you with any experiments you do. They may have some helpful suggestions that will enhance your investigations.

2-1*
The Distance Between Mirror Images

Things you will need:

• 2 plane (flat) mirrors about 10 cm (4 in) on a side

• clay or small heavy objects such as paperweights

• sheet of paper (8-1/2 in x 11 in)

• several long pencils

• ruler

Support two mirrors upright on your bureau or desk. The mirrors should be 30 cm (12 in) apart. Use clay or heavy objects to support the mirrors if necessary. The reflecting surfaces of the two mirrors should face each other as shown in Figure 8. Place an object such as an upright pencil midway between the two mirrors. How many images of the object do you see when you look into each of the mirrors? How far apart are the two nearest images? If you move the object closer to one mirror than the other, will the distance between the two nearest images increase, decrease, or remain the same?

To answer these questions, you may find it useful to first simplify the experiment by using just one mirror to look at one image. Support a mirror upright at the center of a large sheet of paper. Use a small piece of clay to hold a pencil upright at a distance of 10 cm (4 in) from the front of the mirror. The pencil should be taller than the mirror. Look into the mirror where you will see the image of the pencil. Where does the image appear to be? To locate the exact position of the image, you can use what is known as *parallax*.

To find out what is meant by parallax, hold a pencil upright about 30 cm (12 in) or so in front of your face. Close first one eye and then the other. Notice how the pencil appears to change its position relative to more distant objects you can see. Now hold a second pencil about 60 cm (2 ft) in front of your face. Close one eye. Using your other eye, move the two pencils until they lie along the same line of sight. Now close the eye you've been using and open your other eye. As you can see, the two pencils no longer lie along the same line of sight.

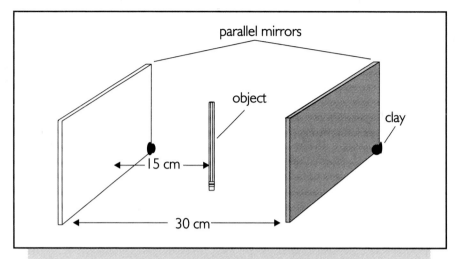

parallel mirrors

object

clay

15 cm

30 cm

Figure 8. How many images do you see when an object is midway between two mirrors whose reflecting surfaces are parallel? How far apart are the first two images seen in each mirror? Does that distance change if the object is moved so that it is closer to one mirror than to the other?

When the two pencils, or any two objects, are at different distances from your eye, they appear to shift relative to each other when seen from slightly different positions such as the positions of your two eyes. This apparent shifting of objects when seen from different positions is called parallax.

Now place one pencil on top of the other so they are both the same distance from your eyes. As you can see, the pencils no longer appear to shift relative to each other when you close first one eye and then the other. There is no parallax between objects that are at the same place.

You can use the lack of parallax to locate the position of an image in a mirror. Place an upright pencil 10 cm (4 in) in front of a mirror on top of a sheet of paper. Move a second upright pencil (taller than the mirror) around behind the mirror until there is no parallax between the top of it and the *image* of the pencil in front of the mirror. Be sure you are looking at the *image* of the pencil in front of the mirror and the *top* of the pencil that is behind the mirror.

(The bottom of the tall pencil behind the mirror is hidden by the mirror.) When there is no parallax between the pencil behind the mirror and the image of the pencil in front of the mirror, the two must be at the same place. Why? You have located the image of the first pencil. Mark the position of the pencil's image on the paper.

Measure the distance between the mirror and the image that you located behind the mirror. How does it compare with the distance between the mirror and the pencil that lies in front of it? Are these distances equal or nearly equal?

Repeat the experiment several times. Each time place the pencil at a different distance from the mirror. Is the distance between a plane mirror and an object always equal to the distance between the object's image and the mirror? (See Figure 9a.)

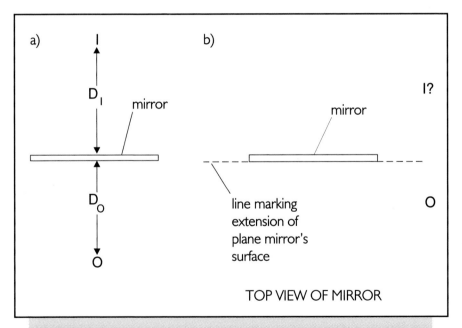

Figure 9. In these drawings, O is the object and I is its image. D_I is the distance between the image, I, and the mirror. D_O is the distance between the object, O, and the mirror. a) Does D_I always equal D_O? b) If an object is at O, where will its image be?

Draw a straight line along the front of the mirror and extend it to either side as shown in Figure 9b. Where is the pencil's image if the pencil is off to one side of the mirror? Can you still locate the image by parallax? Is it as far behind the extended surface of the mirror as the pencil is in front?

Now go back to the original question about an object midway between two plane mirrors. If you move the object closer to one mirror than the other, will the distance between the two nearest images in the two mirrors increase, decrease, or remain the same? Why do you think you see so many images when you look into either mirror? Why do successive images seem to be farther away?

You have used parallax to locate images behind a mirror. Yet, when you look in back of the mirror, you see no image. The images

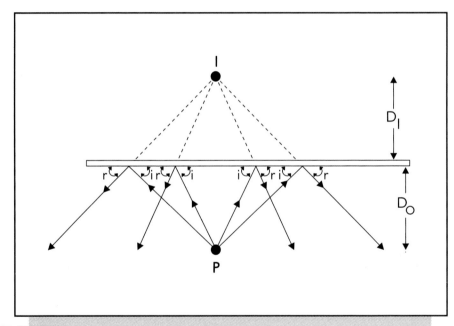

Figure 10. When light rays are reflected, angle *i* always equals angle *r*. Because angle *i* equals angle *r* for all rays of light, light rays from a point P in front of a plane mirror are reflected in such a way that they all appear to come from a point I behind the mirror. This holds true for all points on an object in front of a plane mirror. Can you prove that D_I equals D_O?

28

you see in plane mirrors are called virtual images because they are not real. Unlike the images you see on a movie screen, virtual images can be seen only by looking into a mirror. They exist only because of the way light is reflected from a mirror to our eyes. Figure 10 will help you understand why the virtual images seen in a plane mirror appear to be behind the mirror.

Exploring on Your Own

A mirror is placed against the inside wall of a water-filled aquarium. A small stone rests at a point in front of the mirror. Locate the image of the stone as seen by you looking into the mirror from outside the aquarium. Is the image where you would expect it to be?

2-2*
Colored Lights

Breaking White Light into Colors

As you may know, white light is made up of many different colors. You can easily separate white light into different colors by letting it pass through a diffraction grating. The grating consists of a series of closely spaced slits. When light passes through these narrow slits, it diffracts (spreads out). Because different colors, which have different wavelengths, are diffracted by different amounts, the colors will be spread out into a spectrum after going through the grating. To see the spectrum of colors in white light, look at a glowing straight filament in a clear lightbulb (a showcase bulb works well) as you hold a diffraction grating in front of your eye. Turn the grating until you see the spectrum spread out some distance on both sides of the glowing white filament. What colors do you see in the spectrum?

Cut a narrow slit about 2 mm (1/16 in) wide in the center of a sheet of black construction paper. Tape the paper over the fluorescent tube of a study lamp or bathroom fixture. If necessary, tape additional sheets of the same paper over the ends of the bulb so that the only light from the fluorescent tube comes through the slit (see Figure 11). In a dark room, look at the light coming from the tube through your diffraction grating. Turn the grating until you see a

Things you will need:

- diffraction grating (borrow from your school or buy at a hobby store or science supply house)
- clear bulb such as a showcase bulb or any clear bulb with a single straight filament
- sheet of black construction paper
- tape
- fluorescent tube
- dark room
- adult supervisor
- three light sockets and cords
- electrical outlets
- blue, red, and green lightbulbs
- white or light-colored wall
- short stick

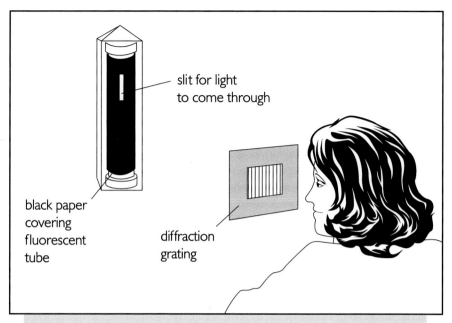

Figure 11. Look at the light coming from a fluorescent tube through a diffraction grating.

spectrum on both sides of the slit. In addition to the white-light spectrum, you will also see bright lines of light. The complete spectrum is caused by the fluorescent coating on the tube. The bright lines are caused by atoms of vapor within the tube. The vapor of each chemical element, when excited by electrical energy, releases specific radiation (colors) characteristic of that element. Record the colors of these bright lines. Then look at Figure 12. Could the vapor in the fluorescent tube be any of those shown in Figure 12? (Some of the lines in a fluorescent-tube spectrum may not be bright enough to be seen.)

Combining Colored Lights to Make White Light

You can also make white light by mixing different colored lights. If you shine red, blue, and green lights all onto the same screen, they will make white light. To see this for yourself, put three light sockets

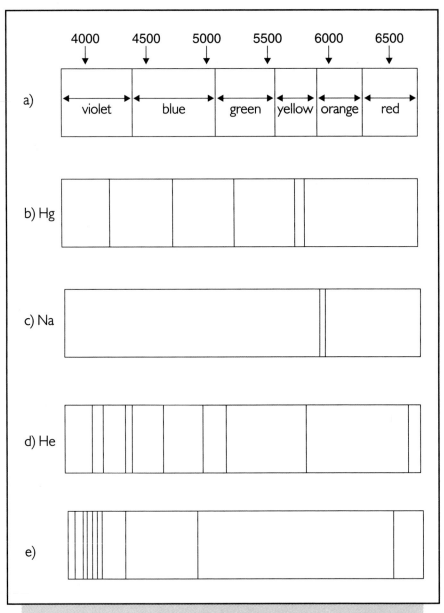

Figure 12. These drawings (b, c, d, and e) show the colored lines seen in the spectra of several glowing elements. They are shown below the complete spectrum (a) found in the light emitted by a glowing incandescent-bulb filament. a) Complete spectrum; b) mercury lines; c) sodium lines; d) helium lines; e) atomic hydrogen lines. The numbers above the complete spectrum show the wavelengths of those points in the spectrum. The wavelengths of the lines in the other spectra can be estimated from those given for the complete spectrum. The measurements are in angstroms (A). An angstrom is 10^{-7} mm, or 0.0000001 mm.

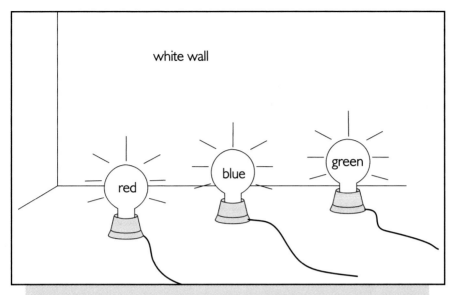

Figure 13. What colors do you see when red, blue, and green lights are mixed on a white wall?

near a white wall in a dark room as shown in Figure 13. **Under adult supervision,** screw a blue bulb into the middle socket. Screw a red and a green bulb into the sockets on either side of the blue bulb.

When all the bulbs are lit, you will see a variety of colors on the wall. A section of the wall in front of the blue bulb where all the colored lights overlap will be white. What color do you see if you turn off the blue bulb and look at the wall where the red and green lights overlap? What color do you see if you turn off the green bulb and look at the wall where the red and blue lights overlap? What color do you see if you turn off the red bulb and look at the wall where the blue and green lights overlap?

Hold a short stick near the wall. How many different-colored shadows will the stick cast if you use one and then different combinations of two colored lights? How many different-colored shadows does the stick cast when all three bulbs are lit? What are the colors of the shadows?

2-3*
Filtered Light

As you saw in Experiment 2-2, white light can be separated into a spectrum of colors, and white light can be made by combining red, blue, and green light. It is also possible to remove certain parts of the spectrum (colored lights) found in white light. That is what colored filters such as those used in theater lighting do.

Look at the world through a red-light filter. What do you see? What do you see through a blue-light filter?

Things you will need:

- red and blue filters (obtain from photography store, drama department, school, or science supply house)

- diffraction grating (borrow from your school or buy at a hobby store or science supply house)

- clear lightbulb

- green, cyan, magenta, and yellow filters (optional)

- red and blue pens or pencils

- black, white, red, blue, and yellow paper

Look at the glowing straight-line filament in a clear lightbulb through a diffraction grating. Now move a red filter in front of the grating. What colors does the red filter remove from the white-light spectrum? What colors does it let through? Do your results agree with the diagram in Figure 14, which shows the light that should come through or be absorbed by a good red filter? If not, what parts of the spectrum does your red filter transmit that a good red filter would not?

Repeat the experiment with a blue filter. What colors does the blue filter remove from the white-light spectrum? What colors does it let through?

If you have green, cyan, magenta, and yellow filters, try to predict what colors of the spectrum each filter will transmit and absorb. Then use a diffraction grating and a clear bulb with a straight-line filament to test your predictions. In how many cases were your predictions correct? How many incorrect predictions did you make?

34

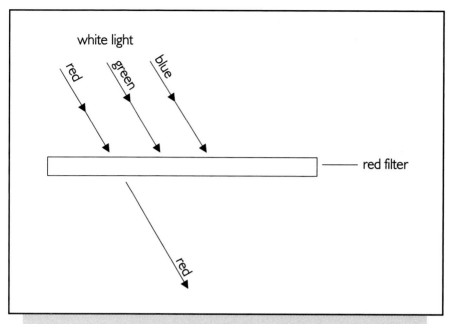

white light

red

green

blue

red filter

red

Figure 14. A red filter transmits red light and absorbs the other colors in white light. What colors will a blue filter absorb and transmit? a green filter?

Try to explain where you made mistakes in reasoning in each of your incorrect predictions.

Place a red-colored pen or pencil and a blue-colored pen or pencil on a sheet of black paper in good even light such as that coming through a north-facing window on a clear day. Predict what you will see if you look at the two colored pens through a red-light filter. Which, if either, pen will be more easily distinguished? Predict what you will see if you look at the two colored pens through a blue filter. Were your predictions correct?

Repeat the experiment with both pens on a white background. Were your predictions correct this time? If not, can you explain why your prediction was incorrect?

Place the red and blue pens on a sheet of red paper. Predict what you will see if you look at the two colored pens through a red-light filter. Which, if either, pen will be more easily distinguished? Were your predictions correct?

Repeat the experiment with the pens on blue paper, and then on yellow paper. Were you able to predict which pen, if either, was more easily distinguished on the blue and yellow papers?

Exploring on Your Own

Investigate spectrophotometry and make your own spectroscope.

2-4*
Pinholes: Images Made by Light Passing Through Small Openings

Perhaps you have heard of pin- hole cameras. Pinhole cameras have no lenses. Instead, they have a tiny opening at the front of the camera that allows a small amount of light to fall on the film at the back of the camera. Because only a small amount of light passes through the pinhole, these cameras are not used for taking action photographs. However, they can produce beautiful still-life photos.

To see how a pinhole camera works, place a light socket with a clear 60-watt bulb on the floor or a counter. Turn a tall card- board box from which the top has been removed upside down

Things you will need:

- light socket
- clear 60-watt bulb
- floor or counter
- large, tall cardboard box
- an adult
- knife
- ruler
- tape
- black construction paper
- pin
- dark room
- sheet of white cardboard or white paper taped to piece of cardboard
- pencil
- thick pin or small nail

and place it over the lightbulb and socket. Be sure the bulb is not close to the cardboard because the bulb will become hot. **Ask an adult** to cut a hole about 10 cm (4 in) wide and 8 cm (3 in) high in one side of the box. The center of the hole should be at approxi- mately the same height as the bulb's filament. Have the **adult** cut a second hole of about the same size on an adjacent side of the box as shown in Figure 15. The second hole should be at a 90-degree angle to the first one.

Tape a piece of black construction paper over one of the 10 cm x 8 cm (4 in x 3 in) holes in the box. Then use a pin to make a tiny hole at the center of the black paper. Turn out all the lights in the

37

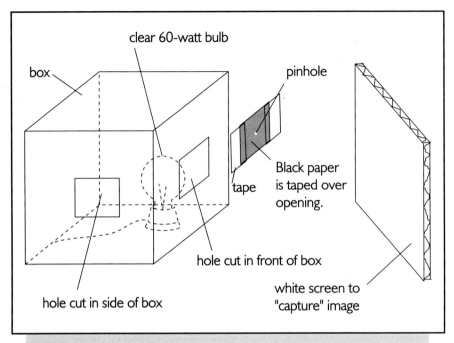

clear 60-watt bulb

box

pinhole

Black paper
is taped over
opening.

tape

hole cut in front of box

white screen to
"capture" image

hole cut in side of box

Figure 15. Pinhole images can be made and "captured" with the materials shown here.

room except for the light inside the box so that the room is quite dark. Make a light screen from a sheet of white cardboard or a piece of cardboard to which you tape a sheet of white paper. Hold the white screen about 30 cm (12 in) from the pinhole, through which a small amount of light shines. What is the source of the light that produces the image on the screen? How can you tell?

What happens to the size of the image as you move the screen farther from the pinhole? What happens to the size of the image as you move the screen closer to the pinhole? Can you explain why the image size changes as it does?

Is the image right side up or upside down? Is it turned right for left? If you have a straight filament, you can still determine whether the image is upside down or turned right for left. Simply reach into the box through the hole in the side and move a pencil slowly up

38

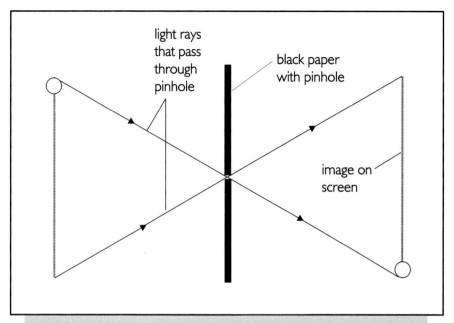

light rays
that pass
through
pinhole

black paper
with pinhole

image on
screen

Figure 16. This drawing shows how light rays from an object pass through a pinhole to form an image. What will happen if a second pinhole is made? What will happen if the pinhole is made bigger?

and down in front of the bulb. You will see the pencil's shadow move across the image on the screen. How can you tell whether or not the image is upside down? How can you find out if it is turned right for left? The drawing in Figure 16 should help you understand how the image is formed. How does the drawing also help you explain why the size of the image changes with the distance from the pinhole? At what distance do you think the size of the image will be the same as the size of the bulb's filament? Why?

Exploring on Your Own

What do you think will happen if you make a second pinhole in the black paper close to the first one? Try it! Were you right? How many images of the bulb's filament do you see now?

39

Use a thicker pin or a small nail to make one of the pinholes wider than the other. What effect does a larger pinhole have on the image? Which image is brighter? Which image is sharper (more distinct)?

What do you think you will see on the screen if you make a dozen or more pinholes in the black paper? Try it! Were you right?

2-5*
Mirror Pinholes: Light Reflected from Tiny Mirrors

Work in a dark room with the same lightbulb and box you used in Experiment 2-4. Remove the black paper with the pinholes that you used to make the images. Place a mirror in front of the hole that was covered with the black paper. Use the mirror to reflect light coming from the bulb onto the white screen you used before. What is the shape of the reflected light pattern? What happens to the size of the pattern of light as you move the screen farther from the mirror?

Things you will need:

- lightbulb and box used in Experiment 2-4
- dark room
- mirror
- white cardboard screen used in Experiment 2-4
- scissors
- black construction paper
- tape
- pencil
- small mirror, such as a pocket mirror
- sun
- nearby building
- distant building

Use scissors to cut a small square about 2 mm (1/16 in) on a side in the center of a piece of black construction paper that is large enough to cover the mirror. Place the paper over the mirror and tape it in place (see Figure 17a). Use the small square area of the mirror that can still reflect light to bounce light coming from the bulb in the box onto the white screen (see Figure 17b). What is the source of the light for the image you see on the screen? How can you explain the image that you see?

Use a pencil as you did in Experiment 2-4 to determine whether the image is upside down or right side up. What do you find? Is the image reversed right for left?

What happens to the size of the image as you move the white screen farther from the mirror? What happens to the size of the image as you move the screen closer to the mirror? Can you explain

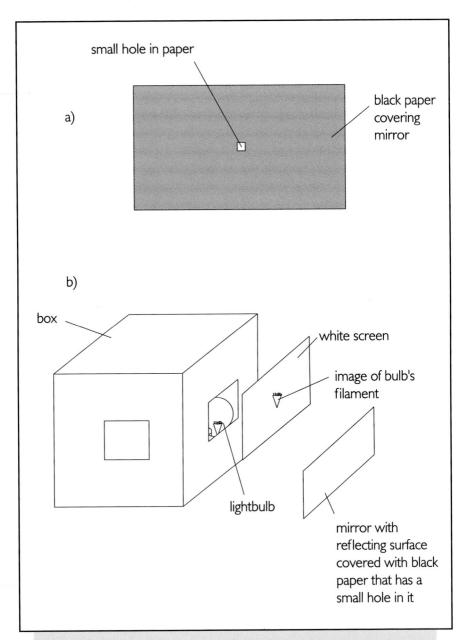

Figure 17. a) A mirror is covered with black paper. Only a square hole 2 mm (1/16 in) on a side allows light to be reflected from the mirror. b) A mirror pinhole image can also be "captured" by reflecting light from the mirror onto a white screen.

why the size changes? Put the screen on the box directly above the filament of the bulb inside the box. Then slowly move the mirror farther from the box, keeping the image on the screen. What happens to the size of the image? Can you explain why?

What do you think will happen if you make a second hole even smaller than the first in the black paper that covers the mirror? Try it! Were you right? How many images of the bulb's filament do you see now? How does the size of the opening to the mirror affect the brightness of the image? How does the size of the opening to the mirror affect the sharpness of the image?

Take a small mirror, such as a pocket mirror, outside on a sunny day. **Do not shine sunlight into anyone's eyes. It can permanently damage his or her eyes!** Use the mirror to reflect light from the sun onto the side of a nearby building. What is the shape of the reflected light pattern? Reflect the sunlight onto a distant building. What is the shape of the light pattern now? What is the source of the image that is being reflected?

Exploring on Your Own

Now that you understand how to make clear pinhole images, build your own pinhole camera. Use the camera to take still-life photographs with black-and-white film.

2-6
Vibrating Rulers and Strings: Sound from Strings

Things you will need:

- 30-cm (12-in) ruler

- desk or table

- ruler that is thicker or thinner than the first one and more rigid or less rigid than the first one

- small block of wood

- stringed instrument (or large rubber band, shoe box, and small block of wood)

Place a 30-cm (12-in) ruler on the edge of a desk or table. Let about half of the ruler extend beyond the edge of the table while you hold the rest of the ruler firmly against the top of the table. Pluck the free end of the ruler. What do you hear?

Move the ruler so that about two thirds of it extend beyond the table. Again, hold the rest of the ruler firmly against the top of the table and pluck the free end. What do you notice about the sound? Is the pitch higher or lower than before?

Now move the ruler so that only about one third of it extends beyond the table. Hold the rest of the ruler firmly against the table-top. What do you predict the sound will be like when you pluck the free end of the ruler? Will the pitch be higher, lower, or the same as the vibrating ruler that was twice as long? Will the pitch be higher, lower, or the same as the vibrating ruler that was 1.5 times as long? Try both! Were you right?

Find a ruler of the same length that is thicker or thinner than the one you have been using. It should feel more rigid or less rigid than the previous one. Place it next to the ruler you used before. Let all but 3 or 4 cm (1–1.5 in) of the rulers extend beyond the edge of the desk or table. Hold the short unextended portions of the rulers firmly against the top of the table or desk. Pluck the free ends of both rulers in turn. Which one vibrates faster? How does the rigidity of a ruler affect its rate of vibration?

With one third of each ruler free to vibrate, predict which one will have the higher pitch when plucked. Pluck each ruler in turn. Was your prediction correct?

Can you adjust the lengths of the free ends of the rulers so that both produce notes of the same pitch? If you can, which ruler has the longer section free to vibrate, the more rigid or the less rigid ruler?

Suppose you support one of the rulers at its midpoint on a small block of wood about 2 cm (3/4 in) wide. Pluck one end of the ruler to make it vibrate. What happens to the other end of the ruler? Does it vibrate as well?

How are the results of this experiment related to musical instruments with strings? If possible, obtain a stringed instrument. Pluck one of the strings. What happens to the pitch of that string when

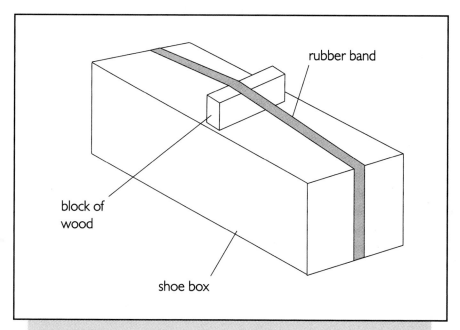

Figure 18. You can make your own one-string banjo from a shoe box, a small block of wood, and a rubber band. Move the block to change the length of the "string."

you shorten the vibrating part of that string by pressing the mid-point of the string against the instrument and then pluck the shortened string?

If you can't obtain a stringed instrument, place a large rubber band around a shoe box as shown in Figure 18. Use a small block of wood to raise the rubber band above the box. Pluck the rubber band. Now shorten the part of the rubber band that you plucked by moving the block. Pluck the shortened part of the rubber band. How does its pitch compare with that of the longer vibrating part?

Exploring on Your Own

See if you can make a one-string banjo on which you can play tunes. Can you make a multistringed instrument and use it to play tunes?

3

Physics in Your Kitchen

The kitchen is an excellent place to do physics experiments. There is usually lots of counter space, hot and cold running water, a sink, stove, and refrigerator, as well as lots of hardware. On the other hand, a kitchen is a busy place, especially before and after meals, so you must be considerate of other people who have to use your "laboratory" for essential tasks. Furthermore, in doing experiments, you may spill water, mess up a sink or counter, or accumulate a bunch of materials needed to carry out an investigation. If you do, be sure to clean up. Put things away so your experiments do not interfere with the work others need to do in the kitchen. Your parents will appreciate it if you do; they may be upset with you if you don't. These words of caution to a wise physicist should be sufficient.

3-1
Archimedes and Your Kitchen Sink

Archimedes, a Greek physicist who lived in the third century B.C., made discoveries that are as relevant today as they were more than two thousand years ago. You can repeat one of his discoveries in your kitchen.

Use a spring balance to weigh a metal object or a lump of clay suspended from a thread. Record its weight in grams. If your spring balance is calibrated in ounces, you can convert ounces to grams—1 ounce is equal to 28.4 grams. Then find the volume of the metal or clay by placing it in a graduated cylinder or measuring cup that is partially filled with water. Of course, the level of the water in the graduated cylinder or measuring cup will rise when you add the metal or clay. How can you find the volume of the metal or clay object? Record that volume.

The density of water is 1.0 gram per cubic centimeter (g/cm^3) or 28.4 grams per ounce. [A cubic centimeter (cm^3) has the same volume as a milliliter (mL).] What weight of water was displaced by the metal or clay object?

Now weigh the metal or clay object while it is submerged in a container of water as shown in Figure 19. How much does the object weigh while suspended in water? What upward (buoyant) force did the water provide the object? How does the buoyant force on the object compare with the weight of the water displaced by the object? The answer to this question was Archimedes' discovery.

Place a container of water on a balance pan or scale. Will the mass of the container increase if you use a thread to suspend a metal or clay object in it? Try it! Were you right? What will be the increase

Things you will need:

- spring balance
- small metal object or lump of clay
- thread
- graduated cylinder or measuring cup
- water
- container
- balance pan or scale

48

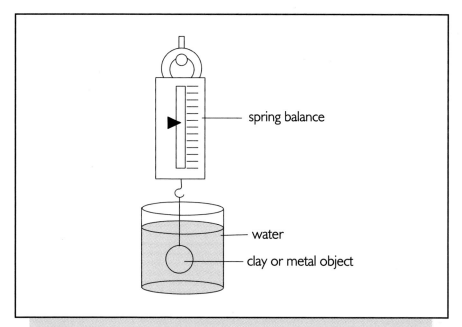

spring balance

water

clay or metal object

Figure 19. What is the weight of the object when it is suspended in water? How much did it weigh while suspended in air? How does its loss of weight in water compare with the weight of the water it displaces?

in the mass of the container of water if you drop the metal or clay object into it?

Will the mass of the container increase if you stick your fingers into the water in the container? Try it! Were you right? How do you explain what you observed?

Suppose an object floats in water. It will weigh zero when suspended from a spring scale and lowered into water. How can you find the buoyant force on an object that floats? How can you find its volume?

3-2*
An Eyedropper and Other "Submarines": Pressure and Buoyancy

Fill a tall, clear glass jar or bottle almost to the top with water. Draw water into an eyedropper and put the filled eyedropper, pointed end first, into the jar. Adjust the amount of water in the eyedropper so that it just floats. The tip of the rubber bulb should be just above the water level in the jar. Put the cork or rubber stopper on the mouth of the bottle or jar as shown in Figure 20, but don't push it down yet.

Things you will need:

- tall, clear glass bottle or jar
- water
- cork or rubber stopper that fits the mouth of the jar or bottle
- glass eyedropper
- condiment packets like those at fast-food restaurants
- jar of water
- plastic soda bottle with screw-on cap

Watch the eyedropper as you gently push the stopper into the bottle or jar. What happens to the eyedropper? What happens when you lift your hand from the stopper? Can you make your "submarine" float midway in the water?

Try to explain what you think makes your submarine work. Watch the water level in the eyedropper when you push down on the stopper. What happens to it? What happens to the water level in the eyedropper when you remove the stopper? How is the operation of your submarine related to Archimedes' discovery?

You can make less transparent "submarines" by using squeeze packets that contain ketchup, relish, mustard, or some other condiment. They are found in abundance at fast-food restaurants. To choose the best packet for a submarine, place a few in a jar of water. The best prospect is a packet that barely floats in water.

Push the chosen packet through the mouth of a plastic soda bottle filled with water. Be careful not to break the packet open. Return the screw-on cap to the bottle and your submarine is ready.

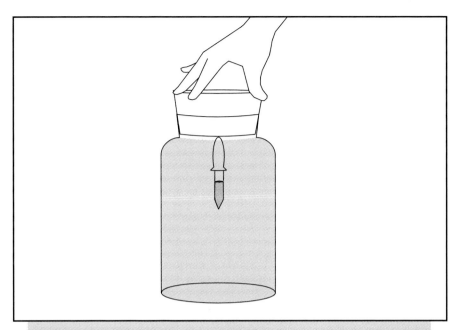

Figure 20. A miniature submarine can be made from a bottle of water and an eyedropper.

What happens when you squeeze the bottle? What happens when you stop squeezing? Can you explain how this submarine works?

Exploring on Your Own

Build a model submarine that will actually travel horizontally under its own power under water. What can you do to control its vertical as well as its horizontal motion?

51

3-3*
A Soda-Straw Balance:
Levers and Balancing

Things you will need:

• plastic soda straw

• paper clips

• straight pin

• 2 small identical tin cans or drinking mugs

• felt-tipped pen

• ruler

• partner

Another discovery of Archimedes involved levers and balances. You can learn much about balances and levers with a simple plastic soda straw and some paper clips.

Begin by placing a pin, like the one shown in Figure 21a, across the space between two small identical tin cans or drinking mugs. Can you balance a soda straw by placing it on the pin?

You probably found it impossible to balance the soda straw by placing it on the pin. Perhaps you can balance it if you push the pin through the straw. Try each of the three pin positions shown in Figure 21b. In which position was it easiest to balance the straw? Will the straw remain balanced if you turn it upside down?

Now that you know how to balance the straw, use a felt-tipped pen to make marks at 1-cm (1/2-in) intervals outward along the straw from its center. Make marks on both sides of the straw. Hang a paper clip at the mark closest to one end of the straw as shown in Figure 21c. (If the paper clip slides along the straw, pinch the clip so that it grips the straw slightly.) Where can you hang a second paper clip to balance the straw? Where can you hang two paper clips to make the straw balance?

Figure 21d shows drawings of one side of three different balanced soda straws. There are two paper clips on the other side of each straw. Use two paper clips to find out how the other side of each soda straw looks. Then make drawings of both sides of the soda straws shown in Figure 21d.

52

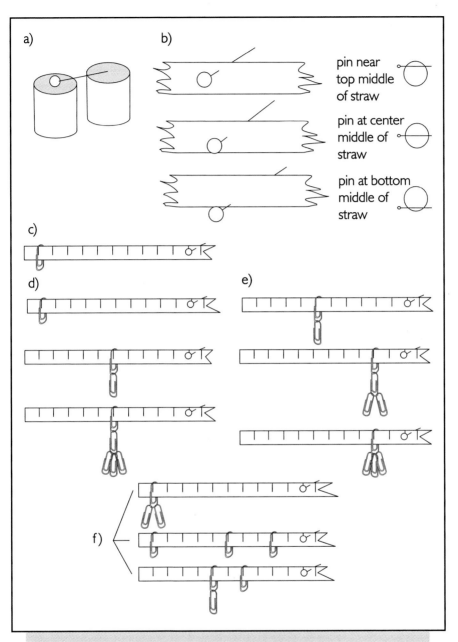

a) A pin is placed across two identical supports.

b)

pin near top middle of straw

pin at center middle of straw

pin at bottom middle of straw

c)

d)

e)

f)

Figure 21. a) A pin is placed across two identical supports. b) In which pin position does the straw balance easiest? c) Hang a paper clip at one end of the straw. Where can you hang a second paper clip to make the straw balance? d) Where are the two paper clips on the other side of these balanced straws? e) Where is the one paper clip on the other side of these balanced straws? f) Where are the two paper clips on the other side of these balanced straws?

Figure 21e also shows three different balanced soda straws. Only one paper clip is on the other side of each straw. Use a single paper clip on the other side of the straw to make the straws shown in Figure 21e balance. Draw a picture of each balanced straw.

In Figure 21f there are two paper clips on the other side of each straw. Determine the possible positions of the two paper clips experimentally. Then draw pictures of the balanced straws.

Play a balance game with a partner. Place paper clips on one side of the soda straw. Give your partner a certain number of paper clips and challenge him or her to place the clips on the other side of the straw and make it balance without moving the paper clips a second time. Then let your partner challenge you. Can the two of you devise a rule that will allow you to make the straw balance for any situation?

Exploring on Your Own

How can you modify your soda straw to make a balance that can be used to weigh small objects?

How is this experiment related to "Seesaw (Teeter-Totter) Physics" in Experiment 5-6 ("Playground Physics") in Chapter 5?

3-4*
A Very Sensitive Soda-Straw Balance

You can make a very sensitive balance, one that can weigh very small objects, by using a soda straw that has its point of support close to one end rather than in the middle. To build such a balance—one like the balance in Figure 22—begin by finding a machine screw that fits snugly into the end of a soda straw. Turn the screw until about half of it is in the straw. Find the approximate balance point of the straw and screw by resting it on your finger. Why does it balance close to the end with the screw?

You will stick a pin through the straw above the approximate balance point. As you know from the previous experiment, the pin should be above the mid-line of the straw. However, to make the balance very sensitive, push the pin through the straw just slightly above the midline. With scissors, cut out about 1 cm (1/2 in) from the top of the straw at the very end of the balance's long arm (see Figure 22). The cut-out section of the straw will serve as your balance pan. It can hold the small things you will weigh. Support the balance by placing the pin on the edges of two short tin cans such as tuna fish cans.

Place some small objects such as a hair, a small piece of paper or foil, an insect's wing, and so on, on the balance pan. Does the

Things you will need:

- soda straw
- machine screw that fits snugly into the end of the soda straw
- straight pin
- ruler
- 2 short tin cans such as tuna fish cans
- small objects such as hair, small pieces of paper or foil, an insect's wing, etc.
- clothespin
- file card
- pencil
- laboratory balance
- meterstick (yardstick)
- fine wire and wire cutter, or sheet of graph paper and scissors
- forceps (tweezers)
- hair of different colors

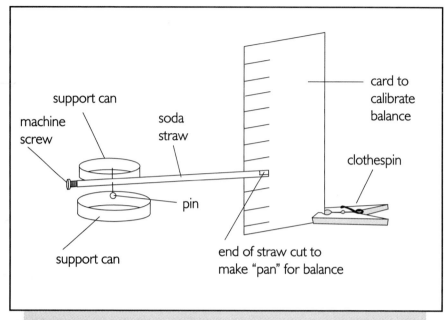

Figure 22. A sensitive balance can be made from a soda straw.

balance respond to such objects? If it doesn't, you may need to move the pin to a point slightly closer to the midline of the soda straw.

Use a clothespin to support a file card in a vertical position close to the balance pan. Use a pencil to mark the position of the balance pan (see Figure 22).

To make a scale for your balance so that you can use it to weigh objects in fractions of a gram, you will have to calibrate it. You can do this by first turning the screw at the short end of the balance until the other end of the beam is tipped slightly upward. Then use a standard laboratory balance, such as one at your school, to weigh a 1-m (1-yd) length of fine wire or a sheet of graph paper. Cut off a 1-cm length of the wire or a single square from the graph paper. Assuming the wire or paper is uniform, how much does the short length of wire or the paper square weigh? Use forceps (tweezers) to put the known weight on the balance pan. It should tip the end of the

56

balance to a slightly lower but distinctly new position. Mark the new position of the balance pan on the file card and label it with the weight you placed on the pan. If the change in the position of the balance pan is too small to measure, or if the balance pan tips by a large amount, you will have to use larger or smaller lengths of wire, finer wire, or more or fewer squares of graph paper until you find a convenient measuring unit of wire or paper.

Once you find the proper weight to tip the beam by a reasonable amount, you can finish calibrating your balance. Simply place one, two, three, four, and so on, units on the pan and make marks on the card to show where the end of the beam is located when these known weights are on the pan. How can you use the calibrated balance to weigh small objects? How many small objects can you find to weigh? How much does each of them weigh?

You might use your balance to compare the weights of different-colored hairs. Choose a standard length of hair that you can weigh on your balance. Then collect blond, black, brown, and red hairs. Cut them to the standard length you chose and weigh them. Is blond hair always lighter or heavier than black hair?

Exploring on Your Own

What other investigations can you carry out with your sensitive balance? Can you find a way to make your balance more sensitive— that is, to make it respond to even smaller weights?

3-5*
Does It Matter Where You Put the Heater?: Heat, Convection, and Density

Things you will need:

Because this experiment involves the use of household electricity, you should work under adult supervision.

Fill a large (12-oz) Styrofoam cup almost to the top with cold water. Use a pencil to mark the water level on the outside of the cup. Rest the bulb of a laboratory thermometer (or a temperature probe connected to a computer) on the bottom of the cup. When the level of the liquid in the thermometer stops moving, record the temperature of the water. Leave the thermometer (or temperature probe) in place. Then hold an

- adult supervisor
- large (12-oz) Styrofoam cup
- cold tap water
- pencil
- laboratory thermometer (or temperature probe connected to a computer)
- electric immersion heater
- clock or watch with second hand
- food coloring
- 2 clear plastic vials
- hot and cold tap water
- eyedropper

immersion heater in the water as shown in Figure 23. The heater coils should be fully immersed but only in the *top* layer of water in the cup. Plug in the heater for exactly one minute. Remove the heater and record the temperature of the layer of water at the bottom of the cup. Raise the thermometer bulb (or temperature probe) to the top layer of water. Record the temperature in the top layer of water after the level of the liquid in the thermometer (or the temperature probe recording) stops changing.

What was the temperature of the water at the bottom of the cup after heating? What was the temperature of the water at the top of the cup? Were they the same? If not, by how many degrees did they differ?

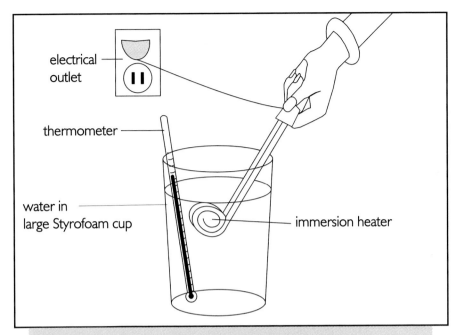

electrical outlet

thermometer

water in large Styrofoam cup

immersion heater

Figure 23. An immersion heater is placed in the top layer of the water that nearly fills a large Styrofoam cup. The bulb of a thermometer rests on the bottom of the cup. For purposes of illustration, the cup is drawn as if it were transparent.

Pour out the water from the previous experiment and fill the cup to the same level as before with cold water. Record the temperature of the water. Again, put the immersion heater into the water. This time let the heater coils rest on the bottom of the cup. Plug in the heater for exactly one minute. Remove the heater and record the temperature of the layer of water at the bottom of the cup. Raise the thermometer bulb (or temperature probe) to the top layer of water. Record the temperature in the top layer of water after the level of the liquid in the thermometer (or the temperature probe recording) stops changing.

What was the temperature of the water at the bottom of the cup after heating? What was the temperature of the water at the top of the cup? Were they the same? If not, by how many degrees did they differ?

Does it matter where you place the heater when you heat water? What difference does it make? Can you explain why?

Perhaps removing the heater stirred up the water and caused a more even distribution of heat and, therefore, of temperature in the second experiment when the heater was on the bottom of the cup. Design an experiment to find out if it was the removal of the heater that caused the more even distribution of heat.

Table 1 provides information about the density of water (the weight per milliliter of volume) at different temperatures. (A milliliter is equal to a cubic centimeter.) Does the information in this table help explain why placing the heater on the bottom of the cup produced a more even distribution of heat?

Table 1: Density of Water at Different Temperatures
(°C = degrees Celsius; g/mL = grams per milliliter, or cubic centimeter)

Temperature (°C)	Density (g/mL)
0	0.9998
4	1.0000
10	0.9997
20	0.9982
50	0.9881
75	0.9749
100	0.9584

As you can see from Table 1, water has its greatest density at 4°C (39°F). The density of ice at 0°C (32°F) is 0.9240. How do these differences in density explain why ice floats? How do they explain why lake water "turns over" before it freezes in the winter? ("Turns over" refers to the fact that water near the bottom of a lake rises to the top while water at the top sinks to the bottom.)

Could the slight differences in density revealed in Table 1 account for the temperature differences between the top and bottom layers of water that you found when you kept the immersion heater in the top layer of water? One way to find out is to put a few drops of food coloring in a plastic vial and then fill the vial with hot tap water. Fill another clear vial with cold water. Using an eyedropper, remove some of the warm colored water from its vial. Place the tip of the eyedropper just below the surface of the cold water in the second vial. Very gently squeeze a few drops of the warm colored water into the top layer of cold water. What happens to the warm water? Does it remain at the top of the cold water, or does it sink to the bottom?

Next, lower the tip of the eyedropper to the bottom of the vial of cold water. Then, very gently squeeze a few drops of the warm colored water into the bottom layer of cold water. What happens to the warm water? Does it remain at the bottom of the cold water, or does it rise to the top?

Do the results of this experiment help explain why placing the immersion heater at the bottom of the water led to a more even distribution of heat than placing it in the top layer of water?

In an electric hot-water tank, where would you expect to find the heater?

When heat is transferred from one place to another by conduction, the flow of heat (as seen by changes in temperature) along a substance occurs without any visible movement of the material itself. Heat is conducted by direct contact of molecules. When one end of a metal bar is heated, the molecules at that end gain kinetic energy (they move faster). The heat is conducted along the metal bar by the collision of the faster-moving (hotter) molecules with the slower-moving ones farther from the source of heat.

When heat is transferred by convection, the fluid (gas or liquid) that is heated moves because of differences in density. For example, warm air flowing from a heating duct on the floor rises toward the ceiling, carrying heat with it.

What do the results of your experiments with the immersion heater indicate about the conductivity of heat by water? Do you think water is a good or poor conductor of heat? Do you think heat in water is transferred better by conduction or by convection? Why?

Exploring on Your Own

Under adult supervision, design and carry out experiments to compare the heat conductivity of water with other substances.

3-6*
Colors from Both Sides of a Soap Film

You have probably noticed the bright colors of a soap bubble dancing in sunlight. Those colors are produced by light reflected from, or transmitted through, the soap film that surrounds the air inside the bubble. You can see those colors more clearly in a soap film as it slowly drains from a thin plastic loop.

You can make the loop from the middle of a plastic lid such as one that covers a coffee can. Use scissors to cut out the loop as shown in Figure 24a. The loop should have an outside diameter of about 5 cm (2 in) and an inside diameter of about

Things you will need:

- plastic lid such as one from a coffee can
- scissors
- ruler
- bubble solution from a store, or you can make your own from dishwashing detergent, sugar, glycerine or wallpaper glue, and warm water
- wide-mouthed container to hold soap solution
- window through which sunlight enters
- newspapers or plastic sheet
- table or stand
- sheet of white paper or cardboard
- cardboard screen

4.5 cm (1.75 in). You can use the bubble solution that is sold for bubble making in toy stores, or you can make your own. To make a soap solution that will produce long-lasting film, add about 80 mL (3 oz) of dishwashing detergent, 10 teaspoonfuls of sugar, and 0.5 teaspoonful of glycerine or wallpaper glue to 500 mL (1 pint) of warm water. Gently stir until thoroughly mixed. Allow to stand in a covered container for three days or longer.

Find a window through which sunlight is entering the room. Place a thick layer of newspapers or a plastic sheet on a table or a stand by the window. Dip the loop you made into the soap solution and hold it in the sunlight. **Do not look at the sun; it can damage your eyes.** If you look at the draining soap film at the

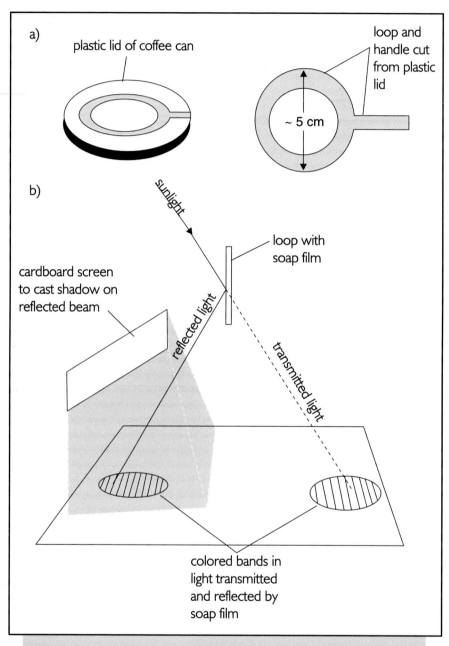

a)
plastic lid of coffee can

loop and handle cut from plastic lid

~ 5 cm

b)
sunlight

loop with soap film

cardboard screen to cast shadow on reflected beam

reflected light

transmitted light

colored bands in light transmitted and reflected by soap film

Figure 24. a) A loop to hold soap film can be made from a plastic lid. b) Colored bands of light reflected and transmitted by the soap film can be seen together on a sheet of white paper. A cardboard screen can be used to cast a shadow on the colors in the reflected beam. This will make it easier to see the colors.

proper angle (off to one side) with your back to the sun, you can see the bright lines of colored light reflected from the soap film. If you look at the film from the other side, again at an angle, you can see the colored bands of light that are transmitted through the soap film.

It is possible to see both the reflected and the transmitted bands of colored light at the same time as shown in Figure 24b. Place a sheet of white paper or cardboard on the covered table by the window. Hold the loop of soap film in the sunlight. By turning it to the proper angle, you will be able to see the light reflected from the soap film on the white paper as well as the light transmitted through the film. A cardboard screen held above the light reflected onto the paper will put the reflected light in a shadow and allow you to see the colors more clearly. By adjusting the position and angle of the loop, the distance between the reflected and transmitted light beams seen on the white paper can be made quite small. This will make it easier for you to see both beams at the same time. When the film finally breaks, you can repeat the process by again dipping the loop into the solution.

Look at the colored bands in the two beams. Are they identical? If you look closely, you will see that when the top band of colored light in the reflected beam is blue, the top band in the transmitted beam is a different color.

Could the corresponding alternate bands of colored light in the two beams be complementary colors? Complementary colors of light are colors that, when combined, produce white light. An explanation of complementary colors of light is given by the color triangle in Figure 25. The primary colors of light (red, blue, and green) are different from the primary colors of pigments (red, blue, and yellow, which are really magenta, cyan, and yellow).

If you haven't already done so, try Experiments 2-2 and 2-3 ("Colored Lights" and "Filtered Light") in Chapter 2. They will help

65

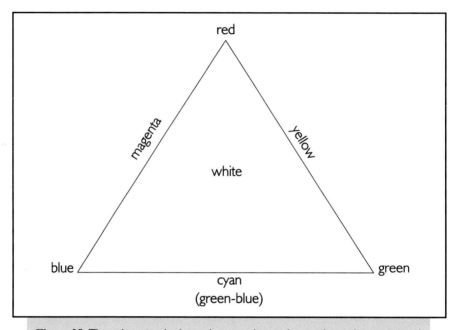

Figure 25. The color triangle drawn here can be used to explain color mixing and complementary colors of light. The combination of the three primary colors—red, green, and blue—at the corners of the triangle produces the white light shown inside the triangle. The combination of two primary colors, such as green and blue, produces the color shown along the side between them. In the case of blue and green, that color is cyan. Combining the color at a corner with the color on the side opposite that corner, such as blue and yellow, produces white light. Blue and yellow are therefore said to be complementary colors. What is the complementary color of red? What is green's complementary color?

you understand the color triangle that shows how complementary colors can be mixed to produce white light.

Exploring on Your Own

Do some research to find out why light passing through thin films produces colored bands. Can similar bands of color be produced by a thin film of air? Can a device be made that uses a thin film to measure very small lengths such as the thickness of a piece of paper or a human hair?

4

Physics in Your Bathroom

Although bathrooms tend to be the smallest rooms in most homes, they do have bathtubs, which offer a large space for doing experiments that require or take place in water. They also have sinks and counter space. Consequently, bathrooms can serve as a laboratory, but remember that bathrooms are usually shared. Try to do your experiments when those with whom you share the room are away.

4-1*
The Coriolis Force and Water down the Drain

You may have heard that because of the Coriolis force, water always spirals clockwise down a bathtub drain in the Northern Hemisphere and counterclockwise in the Southern Hemisphere. You can check up on this idea for yourself. Each time you take a bath, watch the

Things you will need:

- sheet of cardboard
- scissors
- tape
- pen or pencil
- turntable
- sink or bathtub and water

water as it goes down the drain. Does it always spiral clockwise?

The Coriolis force or effect, named for the French physicist Gaspard de Coriolis (1792–1843), is a fictitious force that arises because we live on a spinning sphere (the earth). Since the earth rotates once every 24 hours, a person on the equator moves through one full circumference (40,000 kilometers or 25,000 miles) in 24 hours. This means that person is moving eastward at a speed of

$$\frac{40,000 \text{ km}}{24 \text{ h}} = 1,667 \text{ km/h (about 1,000 mi/h)}.$$

If the same person were standing on the North or South Pole, his or her speed would be zero because he or she is on the axis about which the earth rotates. Someone standing at a point between the equator and one of the Poles moves at a speed somewhat less than the speed at the equator.

A similar effect is true of a disk rotating on a turntable. A point at the center of the disk turns but travels no distance. A point on the edge of the disk travels one full circumference with each rotation. Points between the center and the edge of the disk move at speeds that gradually increase to the maximum speed at the disk's edge.

Now think of a wind moving southward from the earth's North Pole. The wind has no speed to the east. But as it moves south, it flows over land that is moving east (due to the earth's rotation) at ever-increasing speeds. To someone south of the Pole, the wind will appear to move west as well as south. Any wind or long-range missile moving due south in the Northern Hemisphere will appear to curve slowly westward, and any wind or missile moving due north will appear to curve slowly eastward.

You can see a two-dimensional "Coriolis effect" by taping a cardboard disk to a turntable. As the turntable rotates, hold the tip of a pen or pencil at the center of the turntable. Then draw a line straight outward along the cardboard as shown in Figure 26. What does the line actually look like? Is it straight? How can you account for its shape?

If someone is convinced that water always spirals clockwise down a drain in the Northern Hemisphere, partially fill a sink or bathtub

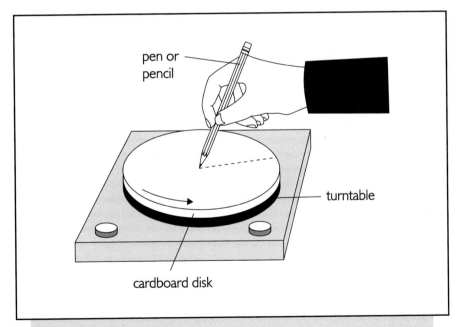

pen or pencil

turntable

cardboard disk

Figure 26. What happens when you draw a straight line on a spinning turntable?

with water. Use your hand to give the water a counterclockwise rotation a few minutes before you invite that person to watch the water empty down the drain. Even though the water will appear to be still, there will be enough residual rotation to make the water spiral counterclockwise down the drain. If someone else is convinced that water always spirals counterclockwise, you can demonstrate clockwise rotation by using the same technique.

As you have seen, the Coriolis effect occurs only when a fluid is moving toward or away from the equator. Furthermore, the effect is evident only for objects or masses of water or air that travel long distances over the earth.

Exploring on Your Own

Now that you understand the Coriolis effect, you might like to build either a Foucault pendulum like one seen in science museums or a model of one. (See *Hands-on Physics Activities with Real-Life Applications* by James Cunningham and Norman Herr, p. 109.)

In the Northern Hemisphere, the plane of swing of a pendulum that swings for a long time, which is what a Foucault pendulum is designed to do, will appear to rotate clockwise. It was probably Foucault's pendulum that led people to believe that water swirls clockwise in the Northern Hemisphere.

4-2
Newton's Third Law in Your Bathtub

The English physicist Sir Isaac Newton (1642–1727) was the first scientist to satisfactorily explain the motion of physical objects. He discovered three laws that explain all motion, whether it be of earthly objects, of satellites orbiting the earth, the sun, or other planets in our solar system, or of the distant stars. Newton's first law states that objects maintain their state of motion or state of rest unless acted on by a force (a push or a pull). His second law deals with what happens when a force, including friction, acts on a body at rest or in motion. The force causes the body to accelerate in the direction of the force. The acceleration will be proportional to the force and inversely proportional to the mass (amount of matter) of the object. This means that doubling the force will double the acceleration, while doubling the mass will halve the acceleration.

Things you will need:
- flexible plastic soda straws
- twist tie
- plastic sandwich bag
- bathtub and water
- food coloring
- sausage-shaped balloon
- aluminum soda can with a pull tab
- string
- nail
- Styrofoam coffee cup
- scissors
- thread

In this experiment, you will be concerned primarily with Newton's third law of motion, which might be called the "push, push-back" law. It states that if one body exerts a force on another, that second body will exert an equal force in the opposite direction on the first body. When you stand on the ground, you exert a downward force due to the earth's gravity. Newton's law simply says that the earth exerts an equal force upward on you; if you push against a wall, the wall pushes back against you with an equal but oppositely directed force. In these examples, nothing moves. But suppose you and a friend are standing on a frozen pond wearing ice

71

skates. You place your hands on your friend's back and give her a gentle push forward. It is not surprising to see your friend accelerate away from you as you push (an effect of the second law) and then slide away at constant speed once you are no longer in contact. But what happens to you? You, too, accelerate as you push because your friend pushes against you with an equal force in the opposite direction—an effect explained by Newton's third law. And, similarly, you move with a steady speed in the opposite direction once contact is broken.

Of course, the "constant" speed is really not constant. Even on ice there is some friction, and friction always acts against motion. Consequently, you and your friend will eventually come to rest unless you push against the ice with your skates in order to change your motion.

One very simple way to see Newton's third law in action is to let a flexible plastic soda straw hang loosely from your lips. Have the short end of the straw turned at a 90-degree angle as shown in Figure 27a. Blow air into the straw. At the bend in the straw, the straw must push the air to the right or left. The air, in turn, according to Newton's third law, must push back on the straw with an equal but oppositely directed force. What do you see that reveals Newton's law in action?

Now use a twist tie to secure a plastic sandwich bag to the free end of the straw. What happens when you blow through the bent straw with the bag attached? Why doesn't the straw move as it did before?

Fill your bathtub with about 6 inches of water. Place a few drops of food coloring in a sausage-shaped balloon. Then fill the balloon with water and place it in the bathtub. Release the neck of the balloon and watch what happens. How is the balloon's motion explained by Newton's third law?

Open an aluminum can with a pull tab. Leave the tab connected to the can. (Don't remove it completely.) Empty the can and attach

72

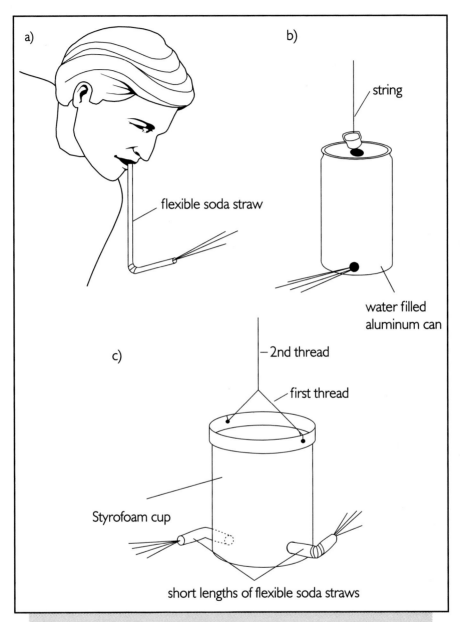

a)

b)

string

flexible soda straw

water filled
aluminum can

c)

2nd thread

first thread

Styrofoam cup

short lengths of flexible soda straws

Figure 27. These are examples of Newton's third law of motion. a) Blow through a flexible straw that has a 90-degree bend in it. b) Let water emerge at an angle from a can suspended at its top center by a string. c) Let water flow from two soda straws bent at 90-degree angles that open into the lower and opposite sides of a water-filled cup.

a string to the tab as close to the can's center as possible. Use a nail to make a hole in the side of the can near the bottom. After inserting the nail, deflect it to one side so that any water in the can will flow out at an angle to the can as shown in Figure 27b. Hold a finger over the hole as you fill the can with water in the bathtub. Then let the can hang from the string as water flows from the can. Which way does the can turn? How is the direction of the can's rotation explained by the third law of motion?

The rotating can is a modified version of Hero's engine. Hero was a Greek engineer who lived in Alexandria during the first century A.D. One of Hero's inventions was a simple steam engine consisting of a hollow sphere with two bent pipes attached to its side. When steam emerged from the pipes, the sphere turned and could be used to do work. Hero had discovered an application of Newton's third law long before Newton but never realized the depth or breadth of his discovery.

You can build an engine similar to Hero's that is powered by water rather than by steam. Use a nail to make two small holes near the bottom on opposite sides of a Styrofoam coffee cup. Cut off the long ends of two flexible drinking straws. Push the bent short ends into the holes you made in the cup as shown in Figure 27c. Make two smaller holes on opposite sides close to the top of the cup. Use a piece of thread to connect those two holes and a second thread to suspend the cup as shown so it can turn freely. Fill the cup with water and hold it over your bathtub. How does this modified version of Hero's engine illustrate a practical use of Newton's third law?

What happens if you turn one straw jet around so that the water jets tend to turn the cup in opposite directions? Can you explain why there is little or no rotation of the cup now?

4-3*
Does Your Weight Depend on Your Position?

Do you think your weight changes when you lie down? When you sit down? To find out, first determine your total weight when it is measured on two bathroom scales with dials, not digital readings. To begin, find your weight by standing first on one bathroom scale and then on the other. The two weighings should agree (or nearly agree).

Next, weigh a strong board that is about as long as you are tall. What is the sum of your

Things you will need:

- 2 bathroom scales with dials (analog, not digital)
- strong board about as long as you are tall
- partner
- small stool or chair
- weight
- spring balance
- thick pillows
- Styrofoam cup
- water
- bathtub
- small nail

weight and the board's weight? Place the board so that one end lies across one bathroom scale and the other end lies across the other scale. Have a partner record the weight registered on each scale when you stand on the board midway between the two scales. How does the sum of the weight readings on the two scales compare with the sum you found before? What happens when you stand closer to one scale than the other? Are the weights recorded on the two scales approximately equal? Does the sum of the two weights change?

Do you think your weight will change when you lie down? Try it! What does your partner find is the weight reading on each scale when you are lying on the board? What is the sum of the two readings? Does your weight change when you lie down?

Do you think your weight changes when you sit down? Design an experiment to find out.

Are you convinced that your total weight doesn't change when you sit or stand or distribute your weight over two different scales? If you are, you might enjoy a surprise about your weight, by employing a method that allows you to lose weight, at least temporarily. While standing on a set of bathroom scales, quickly lower your weight by bending your knees as you watch the dial. What happened to your weight? Now quickly straighten your legs as if you were about to jump. What happens to your weight?

Skiers call the weight losses that you have just seen "unweighting." As a skier's upper body drops, it becomes somewhat like a free-falling body and therefore exerts less force on the skis.

To see the force exerted on a spring by a free-falling weight, first hang a weight from a spring balance. Put some thick pillows below the weight. Then release the spring and watch the dial on the spring scale closely as it and the weight fall. What force does the weight exert on the spring scale as they fall?

As you have seen, a free-falling body is weightless. Here is another way to see the effect of weightlessness. Hold a Styrofoam cup filled with water high above a bathtub. Use a small nail to make a hole in the side of the cup near its bottom. Watch the water flow out of the cup through the hole. Continue to watch the hole as you release the cup and let it fall into the bathtub. What happens to the flow of water through the hole? How can you explain what you saw?

Raising your body as you stand on skis or a bathroom scale is like the beginning of a jump; it takes weight off the skis or scales. In order to jump, however, you must push against the earth. Repeat the experiment on the scale from the bent-knee position, but this time watch the scale closely at the very beginning. What happens to your weight at the moment you first begin to stand erect? What causes this change in weight?

4-4*
Shower Curtain Physics: Heat, Pressure, and Convection

Things you will need:

- shower stall or shower in bathtub
- single lightweight shower curtain
- small feather, light strip of plastic, or candle
- thermometer

Many showers have a heavyweight curtain to avoid the problem you will be investigating. If that is the case, ask a parent or guardian if you may replace the present shower curtain with a lightweight one.

As you shower with the lightweight curtain in place, you will probably find that the bottom of the curtain swings inward. Your task is to try to find the force that causes the curtain to move into the shower. Does it happen only when the water is hot? If so, does lowering the water temperature in the shower reduce the amount the curtain moves inward? Does the rate of water flow from the showerhead affect the movement of the curtain?

To investigate the air currents in the shower, you could use a small feather, a light strip of plastic, or, **with permission from an adult**, a candle flame. You might also like to use a thermometer to measure temperatures at different places in the shower.

Based on your measurements and observations, can you offer a possible explanation (a hypothesis) about why the shower curtain moves inward during your shower? Can you find a way or ways to test your hypothesis?

Exploring on Your Own

Is shower curtain physics related in any way to weather phenomena?

77

4-5
Toilet Physics: Levers, Buoyancy, and Pressure

Things you will need:
- a bathroom toilet

People use toilets every day, but they seldom stop to think about how they work. That's probably because much of the toilet's operating machinery is hidden in the tank at the back of the toilet. **With permission from an adult**, remove the top of the tank and look inside. Among other things, you will see a large spherical float, a chain, a half-spherical valve that lifts to allow water to flow into the toilet, and several other pipes, chains, and levers. Watch what happens inside the tank when you flush the toilet. Can you figure out how a toilet works? Perhaps a plumber will let you watch as he or she installs a toilet in a new building. How is the toilet connected to the water supply? How is it connected to the sewer system?

Note the water level in the toilet's tank. Again, with permission, remove the large spherical float. (You can unscrew it from the rod to which it is attached.) Flush the toilet and wait a few minutes. Why does water continue to flow into the tank after it reaches its normal level? How can you stop the flow? (Hint: lift the rod to which the spherical float was connected.)

Screw the float back onto the rod. What purpose does the float serve?

In a similar way, investigate the role of the levers, chains, handles, pipes, and valves in a toilet.

5

Physics from Playground to Kitchen and Back

There are lots of experiments with a physics flavor that can be done on a playground, an athletic field or court, a lawn, or a vacant lot. As you will see, some of the experiments you can do on a playground are closely related to smaller-scale experiments you can do in your kitchen. One word of caution: Not everyone goes to a playground to do experiments; many people go there just to play and have fun. Be sure you don't let your fun in doing experiments interfere with their fun in playing. If your friends ask what you are doing, they are probably interested in science, too. Perhaps they would like to help you with your investigations.

5-1*
Moving Forward While Falling: Projectiles

If you ride your bike at a steady speed along a level sidewalk, you move horizontally at a steady speed. If you drop a ball, it falls straight down to the ground. But what happens if you drop a ball while you are moving? Does the ball continue to move forward as it falls? Does it fall faster than a ball that is dropped from rest?

To begin this investigation, walk along a hallway or level sidewalk carrying a tennis ball in your hand. Release the ball and continue walking. Does the ball continue to move forward with you as it falls and rebound so that you can catch it as you continue to walk? Or does the ball remain where you dropped it so that you have to stop to catch it? What happens if you stop walking at the moment you drop the ball? Does the ball bounce up where you can catch it, or does it bounce on ahead of you?

Another way to answer this question is to make a bull's-eye with chalk on a level walk or driveway. Then make a water "bomb" by filling a balloon with water

Things you will need:

- hallway or level sidewalk
- tennis ball
- chalk
- balloon
- water
- bicycle
- paper and pencil
- 2 large marbles
- flat ruler
- 2 identical coins
- grooved ruler
- small board
- tacks
- hammer
- small blocks of wood
- box
- sheets of cardboard
- paper
- carbon paper
- partner
- tape
- lawn hose or high-powered squirt gun
- protractor
- level surface, such as a stand, garden table, or seesaw frame
- measuring tape

and tying off the neck. Ride your bike over the bull's-eye as you carry the water-filled balloon in your hand. Release the water bomb when it is directly over the bull's-eye. Does the bomb "explode" on the bull's-eye, or does it continue to move and land ahead of the bull's-eye beside your moving bicycle?

What can you conclude about the motion of a falling object that was moving horizontally when it began to fall? Draw what you believe was the path of the water bomb or the tennis ball that you dropped while moving horizontally.

Does an object that is moving horizontally fall faster, slower, or at the same rate as one that is dropped from rest? To find out, carefully support two large marbles between your thumb and index finger as shown in Figure 28a. Use one finger of your other hand to project one of the marbles horizontally. Because contact between the two marbles is holding them in place, if one is sent off in a horizontal direction the other will fall. Listen carefully as soon as the two marbles begin their different paths to the floor. Do the two marbles hit the floor at the same time, or does one land before the other?

Another way to do this experiment is shown in Figure 28b. Strike the edge of the ruler sharply at the point and in the direction indicated by the arrow. The coin resting on the ruler will fall straight down to the floor; the coin on the table will be projected horizontally. Again, listen carefully. Do the two coins hit the floor at the same time, or does one land before the other? What can you conclude about the rate of fall of the two objects?

The Path of a Projectile

To see if your drawing of the path of a falling object that is also moving horizontally is similar to an actual path, you can map the path of a marble in such a fall. To do this, let a marble roll down a grooved ruler as shown in Figure 29. The ruler is fastened to a small board with tacks hammered into the board. It is curved to make a ramp by placing a block of wood under the ruler as shown. The

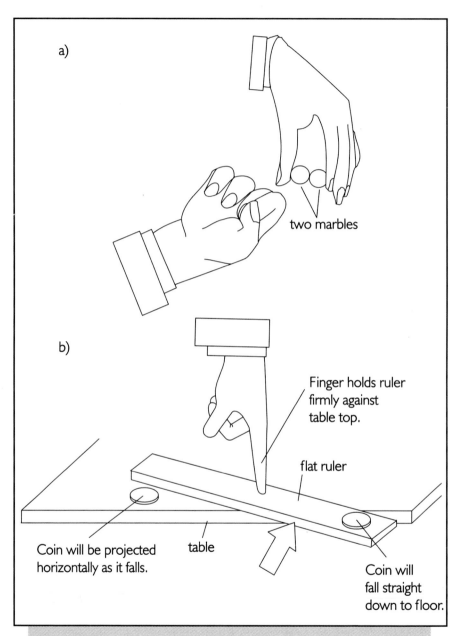

a)

two marbles

b)

Finger holds ruler
firmly against
table top.

flat ruler

Coin will be projected
horizontally as it falls.

table

Coin will
fall straight
down to floor.

Figure 28. Does an object that is moving horizontally as it falls fall at the same rate as one that falls straight down? a) One way to find out is to use two marbles. b) Another way to find out is to use two coins.

grooved-ruler launcher is put on a level elevated surface so that the marble can fall as it moves horizontally after leaving the end of the ruler. A sheet of cardboard next to the front of the end of the ruler will allow you to map the marble's path.

Always start the marble at the top of its "launching pad." A sheet of carbon paper placed face down over a sheet of white paper can be used to mark the landing point of the marble. Mark the landing point and the point where the marble leaves the ruler on the vertical sheet of cardboard. With a pencil, make a rough sketch of the path you think the marble follows during its flight. Compare the sketch with the actual path by watching the marble from the side as it travels from the end of the ruler to the point where it lands. It will help if a partner releases the marble at the top of the launching ramp while you watch its flight through the air from the side. Keep watching, launching, and mapping until you have drawn a path that

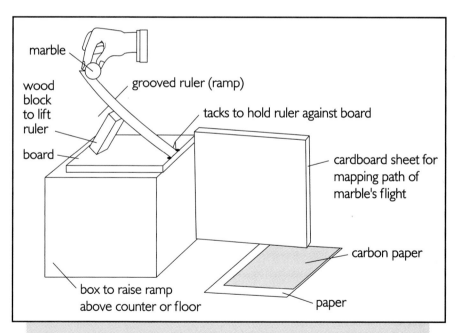

Figure 29. This device can be used to map the path of a marble projectile launched from the end of a grooved ruler.

matches the path followed by the marble. You will know you have succeeded when the marble, in its flight, follows the path marked on the cardboard sheet.

If you have difficulty, rest another sheet of cardboard horizontally on blocks at different levels below the end of the ruler. By placing carbon paper on white paper taped to the horizontal cardboard, you can mark the position where the marble lands at different points along its flight to the floor or counter. These points can then be marked on the vertical sheet of cardboard.

How will the path of the marble change if you tip the end of the ramp upward? If you tip the end of the ramp downward?

Water Projectiles

You can take these experiments with projectiles (that's what we call objects that are projected so that they move both vertically and horizontally) back to the playground or lawn. There you can use a lawn hose or a high-powered squirt gun that uses compressed air to launch water missiles in rapid sequence. In addition to seeing the path of the projectiles, you can investigate the range of these projectiles launched into the air at different angles. Use a sheet of cardboard to build a large half-protractor as shown in Figure 30. Place the giant protractor on a level surface, such as a stand, garden table, or seesaw support so that you will know the angle at which you launch the water projectiles. Of course, speed also affects the range of projectiles, so you want to be sure the speed at which the water emerges from the water gun or hose is the same for each angle. You can do this by marking the point where the water lands when it is fired horizontally from the level surface on which you place the protractor. Test several times to be sure that point is approximately the same each time before projecting the water at different angles.

After establishing the fixed range for 0 degrees, launch the water at an angle of 10 degrees. Have a partner mark the point where

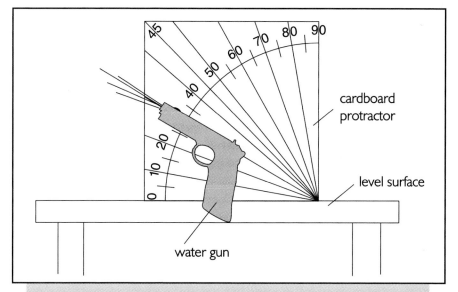

Figure 30. What angle of launch gives the maximum range for projectiles? The water gun shown here is being fired at an angle of 30 degrees.

the water lands. The distance from the launch site to the point where the water lands is the range for that angle. Repeat the experiment for 20, 30, 40, 45, 50, 60, 70, 75, and 80 degrees. Why might it be wise to skip 90 degrees?

For which angle is the range greatest? Are there angles for which the range is very nearly or exactly the same? If there are, what are these angles?

Exploring on Your Own

Find out how falling objects accelerate as they fall. Use that information to determine how long it takes for a projectile launched from a ramp such as the one in Figure 29 to reach the floor. Use that information together with the horizontal distance the projectile travels to determine its horizontal velocity. Then use all your information to map the projectile's expected path at 0.05s intervals. Compare the map you have made with the actual path of the projectile. How closely do they agree?

5-2*
How Does the Speed of a Falling Object Change?

Of course, a falling object changes speed as it falls. When you release it, its speed is zero, so its speed must increase. But how? Does it suddenly reach a constant speed and then fall at that rate? Or does its speed gradually increase as it falls—that is, does it accelerate as it falls? To find out, you can use a stopwatch or make a rough measurement of the time for a ball to fall different distances by counting to five ("one, two, three, four, five") as fast as possible. It should take about one second to count rapidly to five. One way to test this time measurement is to count to five as fast as you can ten times. It should take 10

Things you will need:

- stopwatch (not essential)
- ball
- meterstick, yardstick, or tape measure
- notebook
- pencil or pen
- an adult
- height of 4 m (such as a second-story window) from which to drop a ball
- graph paper
- piece of heavy string about 3 m long
- heavy spike or bolt
- 4 heavy washers or nuts
- wide board (if experiment is done on wooden floor)
- paper clips

seconds. You can check up on this by using a clock or watch with a second hand to measure the time as you count. If a count of five takes 1 second, each count corresponds to 1/5 second (0.2 second).

Hold the ball 1 m (3 ft 3 in) above the floor. Start the stopwatch or begin counting the instant you release the ball. Stop the watch or stop counting at the moment the ball strikes the floor. Record your results in a notebook. Repeat your measurements several times until your measurements are consistent. (It takes a little time to get the hang of starting and stopping the watch or count.) Next, drop the ball from a height of 2 m (6 ft 6 3/4 in). If the ball falls at a steady speed, it should take twice as long to fall 2 m as it did to fall 1 m. How long does it take for the ball to fall 2 m? Does it take the ball twice as long or less than twice as long to fall 2 m? What does this tell you?

If possible, **ask an adult** to help you measure the time for a ball to fall 4 m (13 ft 1 in). Dropping the ball from a second-story window will probably provide the height you need. How long does it take the ball to fall 4 m? Is this twice the time it took to fall 2 m? Is it four times the time it took the ball to fall 1 m? What do these measurements tell you? Do you think the ball falls at a steady speed, or do you think it accelerates (increases its speed)? Why?

Suppose you find that the times for a ball to fall different distances are similar to the results shown in Table 2.

Table 2: Times for a ball to fall different distances

Distance fallen (meters)	Time to fall (seconds)
1.0	0.45
2.0	0.65
3.0	0.78
4.0	0.90

Data like those in Table 2 suggest that the ball accelerates as it falls. In fact, the data indicate that when the time doubles, the ball falls not twice as far but four times as far. (Notice that the time to fall 4 m was only twice as long as the time to fall 1 m.) The number 2 squared (2 x 2, or 2^2) is 4. Is it possible that the distance fallen is proportional to the square of the time to fall?

One way to test this idea is to plot a graph with distance on the vertical axis and the square of the time on the horizontal axis. You can do this very easily. In a notebook, record the data shown in Table 2, leaving room for a third column in which you record the square of the time. For example, the square of 0.45 s is 0.20 s^2. Next, plot the data for distance (on the vertical axis) versus time squared (horizontal axis) on your graph. Do the same for the data you collected. What do you conclude?

Another way to test this idea is to let objects fall simultaneously from heights that are related as the squares of 1, 2, 3, 4, and so on—that is, heights of 1, 4, 9, 16, . . . units of distance. If objects really do fall through distances that vary with the square of the time to fall, then if the objects are released at the same moment, we should hear them hit the floor in equally spaced time intervals. On the other hand, if objects fall at constant speed, they will hit the floor in equally spaced time intervals when they fall through equally spaced heights—that is, intervals of 1, 2, 3, 4, and so on.

You can build a device to see whether or not objects fall through distances that are related as the squares of their times to fall. Tie one end of a piece of heavy string about 3 m (3.3 yd) long around a heavy spike or bolt. Slide four heavy washers or nuts to serve as weights onto the string and let them slide down to the spike or bolt. Have an **adult** help you tie the other end of the string to something at least 2.4 m above a concrete floor. (If the experiment is done on a floor in a house or school, place the spike or bolt on a wide board so you will not damage the floor.) Use paper clips to support the washers or nuts at heights of 15 cm, 60 cm, 135 cm, and 240 cm (6 in, 24 in, 54 in, and 96 in) above the bolt or spike resting on the floor as shown in Figure 31a. As you can see, the heights of the second, third, and fourth weights are 4, 9, and 16 times as high as the first weight is above the floor or board. Consequently, the heights of the weights that will fall to the floor are, relative to the height of the first weight, in the ratios of 4:1, 9:1, and 16:1. If the heights that objects fall really are related to the squares of the times required to fall, you should hear the weights hit the floor at equally

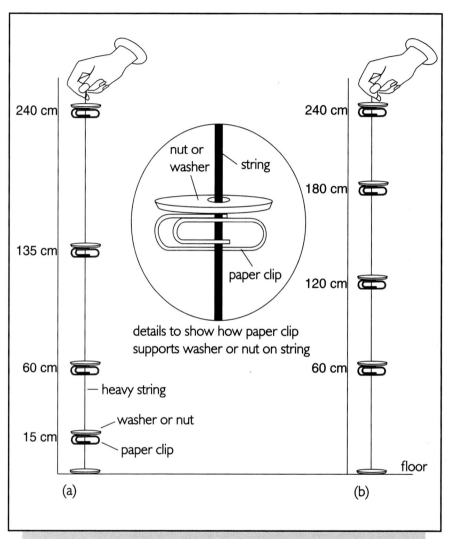

Figure 31. a) If height of fall is related to the square of the time to fall, then washers dropped from height ratios of 1:4:9:16 should strike the floor at equally spaced time intervals if released simultaneously. b) If height of fall is directly related to the time to fall (constant speed while falling), then washers at height ratios of 1:2:3:4 should strike the floor at equally spaced time intervals.

spaced intervals of time when the **adult** releases the top of the string. What do you hear when this happens? Does the height through which an object falls appear to be related to the square of the time on the basis of what you hear?

On the other hand, if objects fall at a constant speed, the heights of fall should be in the same ratio as the times to fall because at constant speed an object travels twice as far in twice the time. To test this idea, support the washers or nuts at 60-cm (2-ft) intervals as shown in Figure 31b. When the **adult** releases the string and these weights fall, do they hit the floor at equally spaced time intervals?

Exploring on Your Own

The Italian physicist Galileo (1564–1642) approached the problem of timing falling objects in another way. He "diluted" gravity by having balls roll down an inclined plane instead of falling freely. Why did he call it "diluting gravity"? See whether you can devise a way to dilute gravity in order to measure the times required for objects to "fall" through different heights.

Do you think a heavy ball falls at a faster rate than a lighter one? Design an experiment of your own to find out.

5-3*
How Does Air Affect a Falling Object?

Drop a tennis ball and a baseball from the same height at the same time. As you can see, they will fall side by side to the floor even if you release them at the ceiling. This shows that the rate at which objects fall does not depend on their weight. In a vacuum a piece of paper, a baseball, and a book would all fall at the same rate. But suppose you hold a sheet of paper horizontally in one hand and a book in the

Things you will need:

- tennis ball
- baseball
- sheets of paper
- book
- 2 nickels
- 2 index cards
- plastic tape
- coffee filters
- stopwatch (optional)
- meterstick or yardstick

other at the same height in the air above the floor in a room. Release both objects at the same time by quickly lowering your hands and pulling them out of the way. Which object reaches the floor first?

Friction between the air and the paper must be enough to reduce the rate at which the paper falls. But suppose you put the paper on top of the book so that its edges do not project beyond the book. Then the air cannot get underneath the paper. Now drop the book. Do paper and book fall together?

Does the surface area of the paper exposed to the air have any effect on the rate at which the paper falls? To find out, squeeze the paper tightly together into a small ball. Drop the paper ball and a book from the same height at the same time. How do their rates of fall compare?

Another way to look at the effect of surface area on falling bodies is to drop two sheets of paper, held horizontally, at the same time. One sheet is open, the other sheet is folded in half. Which sheet falls faster?

91

Repeat the experiment, but this time compare the rates of fall for a sheet that has been folded once with a sheet that has been folded twice. Continue to do this, each time with a sheet that has been folded one more time than the other. How many times can you fold a sheet of paper? What does the folding tell you about the effect of surface area on the rate of fall?

Tape a nickel to the center of an index card. Tape another nickel close to the end of another index card. Hold each card in a horizontal position. If you drop the two cards at the same time, will they fall together or will one fall faster than the other? Try it! Did you correctly predict the way they fell? Can you explain why they fall the way they do?

Terminal Velocity of Falling Objects

Sometimes falling objects reach a constant speed, called their terminal velocity, quite quickly. Sheets of paper would fall at constant speed if they didn't twist and turn and change their orientation so much as they fall. One paper product that does fall without great changes in its orientation is a coffee filter. Try dropping a coffee filter in its right-side-up position—the orientation it has when in the coffeemaker. As you can see, it falls quite smoothly without twisting and turning.

To find out if a coffee filter reaches terminal velocity almost immediately, you can use a stopwatch or the fast counting method used in Experiment 5-2 ("How Does the Speed of a Falling Object Change?") to find its rate of fall through different heights. You might start by measuring the time for a coffee filter to fall 1.0 m (39 3/8 in). Repeat your measurements several times until your measurements are consistent. (It takes a little time to get the hang of starting and stopping the watch or count.) How can you find the filter's average speed during its fall?

Next, measure the times for the coffee filter to fall 0.5 m (19 11/16 in), 1.5 m (4 ft 11 in), 2.0 m (6 ft 6 3/4 in), and perhaps even greater heights if you have high ceilings. You will need an **adult** to help you with the greater heights. For each height, find the average speed at which the coffee filter falls. Are all the speeds very nearly the same? If they are, what does that tell you about the time for the filter to reach its terminal velocity? If the speeds are not all the same, can you tell about how far or how long the filter falls before reaching a terminal speed?

What do you think will happen if you place one filter inside a second and drop the two together? Will the speed of fall double? Will it take longer to reach a terminal velocity? What happens to the speeds and terminal velocities if you drop three filters? Four filters?

Exploring on Your Own

Do some research at your library or on the Internet to find out more about terminal velocity. Try to measure or read about the terminal velocities of objects that fall through air such as feathers, leaves, paper, dust particles, and sky divers.

5-4*
Curveballs

Sir Isaac Newton was a tennis player as well as perhaps the world's greatest scientist and mathematician. He would have had no difficulty believing that a baseball pitcher can throw a curveball because Newton knew

how to make a tennis ball curve. He said that a ball curves because it is spinning as it moves forward and you can control the direction it curves by the way you make it spin. Newton reasoned that a ball curves because the side of the ball that is spinning into the air as the ball moves forward collects more particles of air on its rough surface than the side that is spinning away from the air into which

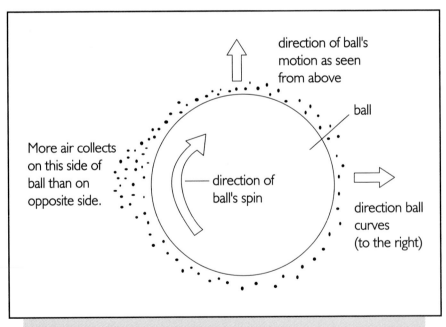

Figure 32. Sir Isaac Newton explained that a ball curves because the air pressure becomes greater on one side than on the other.

94

the ball is moving (see Figure 32). Because more air particles push against one side of the ball than the other, the side with more air "feels" a greater pressure on it than the opposite side, so it gets pushed from the higher pressure toward the lower pressure, causing it to curve off its straight-line course.

You can make a beach ball curve very easily because it is light and has a large surface on which air can accumulate and so increase the pressure. Hold the beach ball in both hands. As you push it forward with both arms give the ball a sideways spin (about a vertical axis) with your hands by pulling one hand backward and pushing the other hand forward just as you release the ball. Watch the ball closely. Does it curve the way Newton predicted it would? (Of course, the ball also falls; you can't remove gravity.) How can you make it curve in the opposite direction?

Repeat the experiment a number of times. Watch what happens when you give the ball a clockwise spin as you release it; then watch when you give it a counterclockwise spin. If you are a baseball player, perhaps you can make a baseball curve by turning your wrist as you release the ball.

Do you play tennis? If you do, see if you can make the tennis ball curve when you serve it as Newton did, by applying spin to the ball when you hit it with the racket. Do you play basketball? If you do, how can you make a bounce pass move to the right or left after the bounce by putting spin on the ball?

5-5*
Newton's Law and Bouncing Balls That Spin

Things you will need:

• beach ball

• smooth level surface or floor

• baseball (optional)

• tennis ball and racket (optional)

• basketball (optional)

This experiment is another example of Newton's third law of motion, which you encountered before in Experiment 4-2 ("Newton's Third Law in Your Bathtub"). As you may remember, this law states that if one body exerts a force on a second body, that second body will exert an equal force in the opposite direction on the first body.

With Newton's third law in mind, try experimenting with a spinning beach ball that you bounce on a smooth level surface such as a basketball or tennis court or any other level surface or floor. Give the ball some backspin (make it spin toward you) as you release it so that it falls straight down to the floor. When it strikes the floor, which way does it bounce—toward you, away from you, or straight up?

Repeat the experiment, but this time give it some forward spin (away from you) as you release it so that it again falls straight down to the floor. Which way does it bounce this time?

To understand why the spinning ball bounces the way it does, think about Newton's third law and the way the spinning ball strikes the floor. Figure 33 may help you with this analysis.

Now give the ball backspin at the same time you bounce it forward as you would to make a bounce pass in basketball. How does the backspin affect the ball's path? How will forward spin applied to a ball affect a bounce pass? What can you do to make a ball bounce sideways?

Apply what you have learned with a beach ball to the balls used in sports. How does spin affect the behavior of a tennis ball? Of a

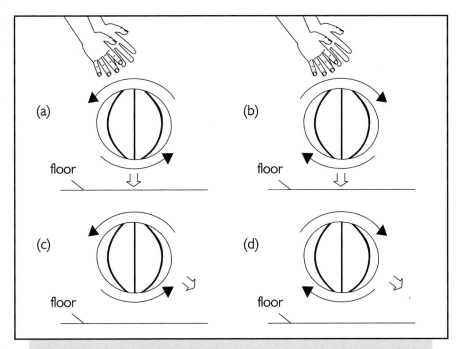

Figure 33. a) A falling ball with backspin is about to strike the floor. Because of its spin and the friction that will exist between ball and floor, which way will the ball push against the floor (other than downward)? Which way will the floor push against the ball? How will the floor's push on the ball affect its upward bounce? b) Use a similar analysis to explain the bounce of this ball, which has forward spin. c) and d) How will the spin of each of these balls affect their bounce?

baseball? How does spin affect a basketball on the court, the backboard, and the rim of the basket? How are the paths of other balls used in various sports affected by spin?

Exploring on Your Own

A Superball is not used in sports, but you can find some very strange behavior by bouncing a spinning Superball. Can you explain what you observe?

5-6*
Playground Physics

The playground is a good place to carry out a lot of physics experiments. There are slides, swings, seesaws (teeter-totters), whirligigs (miniature merry-go-rounds), and lots of space. You can experiment with all of them.

Swinging Physics: A Swing Pendulum

Have a friend sit on a swing. He or she is to do nothing—no pumping—just sit. Give your friend a small push. Then use a stopwatch or a watch with a second hand to find out how long it takes your friend to make ten oscillations. A complete oscillation is the movement from one end of the back-and-forth motion to the other end and back again. What is the period of the swing (the time to make one complete oscillation) with your friend seated on it? Why is it more accurate to measure the time to make ten oscillations rather than just one? How can you find the period (the time to make one oscillation)?

Next, give your friend a harder push so that he or she swings through a greater distance. Again, measure the time to make ten

Things you will need:

- friend
- playground swings
- stopwatch or watch with a second hand
- people of very different weights
- playground slide
- waxed paper
- newspaper, brown paper, aluminum foil, plastic wrap, etc.
- seesaw (teeter-totter)
- bathroom scale with a dial
- measuring tape, yardstick, or meterstick
- chalk
- 2 friends
- pencil and pad or notebook
- miniature merry-go-round, whirligig, etc.
- tennis ball
- accelerometer
- table or counter

complete oscillations. How does amplitude (distance the swing moves) affect its period?

Ask someone who is much heavier or lighter than your friend to sit on the same swing. How does the weight of the person on the swing affect the swing's period?

Finally, ask your friend to sit on a swing that is much longer (from points of support to seat) than the swing he or she was on before. Again, measure the period of the swing by timing ten oscillations. Then repeat the experiment with your friend on a swing that is much shorter than the first one you used. Does the length of a swing affect its period? If so, how is its period affected?

Sliding Physics: Friction on a Playground Slide

Have your friend slide down a playground slide. He or she should be able to go down the slide without having to push to get started. Use a stopwatch or count from one to five as fast as you can to find out how long it takes your friend to go down the slide. See Experiment 5-2 ("How Does the Speed of a Falling Object Change?") to learn how you can use rapid counting to measure time.

Have your friend repeat the experiment while sitting on a large sheet of waxed paper. How does waxed paper affect the frictional force between your friend and the metal surface of the slide? How can you tell?

Repeat the experiment with your friend seated on other surfaces such as newspaper, brown paper, aluminum foil, plastic wrap, and so on. How do these surfaces affect the friction between your friend and the slide?

Design and carry out an experiment to find out how the weight of the person on the slide affects the friction between the person and the slide. Design and carry out an experiment to find out how the surface area in contact with the slide affects the friction between person and slide.

Seesaw (Teeter-Totter) Physics

Find a seesaw that is balanced at its center point of support. Have a friend stand on a bathroom scale that is resting on a solid level surface. Record his or her weight. Use a measuring tape, yardstick, or meterstick to measure the distance from the center of the seesaw to a point about one third of the distance out to one end. Record that distance and mark the point with chalk. Ask your friend to sit there, while another friend pushes on the other end of the seesaw to keep the beam balanced. Place the bathroom scale on the opposite side of the beam at the same distance from the center as your friend (see Figure 34). Push on the scale until your force on the scale is enough to balance your friend on the other side of the beam. How does the force you exert (shown on the scale) compare with your friend's weight?

Figure 34. Experimenting on a seesaw

Next, place the bathroom scale at various distances from the center of the beam. Balance your friend by pushing on the scale at each location. Record the distance and force at each location on a chart like the one below. Some sample data are given in the chart below. Your data will probably be different.

Weight of friend on the board	Friend's distance from board's center	Distance of force from board's center	Force needed to balance friend
100 lb	2 feet	2 feet	100 lb
100 lb	2 feet	3 feet	65 lb
100 lb	2 feet	4 feet	50 lb
100 lb	2 feet	5 feet	40 lb
——	——	——	——
——	——	——	——
——	——	——	——

Now have your friend move to one or more new positions, such as half or two thirds of the distance from the center to the end of the beam, and repeat the experiment. You may have to have your friend or an adult help you push on the scale to make the beam balance for some of these experiments.

Study the data carefully. Can you find a pattern in the numbers? For each set of numbers, how does the product of your friend's weight multiplied by his or her distance from the center of the board compare with the product of the force you exert and the distance of the scale from the center of the beam?

Some seesaws are adjustable; you can make one side of the seesaw longer than the other side. Why would you want to make one side longer than the other?

On a seesaw that is balanced at its midpoint, where would you sit to balance someone who weighs much less than you and who is seated on the far end of the seesaw? What adjustments would you make if you wanted to balance a seesaw when someone much heavier than you is seated on the opposite side?

How could you use what you have learned on the seesaw to build a balance that you could use to weigh small objects in a laboratory? How is this experiment related to Experiment 3-3 ("A Soda-Straw Balance")?

Merry-Go-Round Physics

Many playgrounds have miniature merry-go-rounds, sometimes called whirligigs or other names, like the one shown in Figure 35. If you sit on the outer edge of the miniature merry-go-round while it is turning, you can see some of the Coriolis effects described in Experiment 4-1 ("The Coriolis Force and Water down the Drain"). Have someone kneeling at the center of the merry-go-round roll a ball outward toward you while you both spin slowly. What path does the ball follow on the merry-go-round floor? What path does it follow if viewed from outside the merry-go-round?

Use a tennis ball to play catch with someone seated on the opposite side of the merry-go-round when both of you are rotating slowly. Play some more catch when you are both rotating more rapidly. How can you throw the ball so your partner can catch it? Try to play catch by rolling the ball across the merry-go-round floor. What path does the ball follow? How can you roll the ball so your partner can catch it?

Detecting Acceleration

While you may not be aware of it, you are accelerating when you ride a merry-go-round, even though you may be rotating at constant speed. The best way to detect this acceleration is to hold an accelerometer as you ride the merry-go-round. Accelerometers

Figure 35. Circular-motion experiments can be done on a miniature merry-go-round.

come in a variety of types and sizes. Figure 36 shows you how to build three different kinds.

Once you have built one or more of the accelerometers, you can do a simple experiment to see how they work. Place the accelerometer on a table or counter and move it along the surface with your hand so that its speed increases as it goes. How does each of the accelerometers you tested indicate an acceleration? How does it indicate a deceleration (a decrease in speed), or negative acceleration?

In which of the accelerometers you tested does the indicator move in the direction of the acceleration or deceleration? In which accelerometer does the indicator move in a direction that is opposite the direction of the acceleration or deceleration?

Take one or more of your accelerometers for a ride on a merry-go-round that is turning at a constant rate. According to the

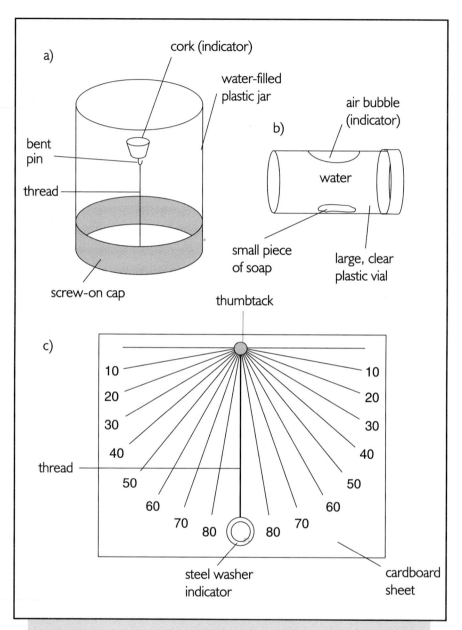

Figure 36. All of these accelerometers should be kept level when in use. In all three, the indicator gives the direction of the acceleration. a) A cork in an inverted water-filled jar is one kind of accelerometer. b) A bubble accelerometer consists of a large, clear water-filled plastic vial with enough air to make a bubble. The small piece of soap reduces surface tension so that the bubble will move more easily. c) A cardboard sheet accelerometer has a steel washer suspended from a thread supported by a thumbtack or pushpin.

indicator, what is the direction of your acceleration as you ride on the merry-go-round? Does the acceleration increase or decrease as you move closer to the center of the merry-go-round? As you move farther from the center? How can you tell?

In the following experiment you will see why you were told to keep the speed of the merry-go-round constant as you examined the direction and size of the acceleration. To find out how the rate at which the merry-go-round turns affects your inward acceleration, you should keep the accelerometer at one position on the merry-go-round. Why? How does your inward acceleration on the merry-go-round change if the merry-go-round turns faster? If it turns slower?

Exploring on Your Own

Design, build, and calibrate an accelerometer that will actually measure the magnitude (size) of accelerations. Since acceleration is change in velocity per time (velocity change ÷ time), the accelerometer will have to be able to measure both changes in velocity, which have units such as miles per hour (mi/h) or meters per second (m/s), and time, which might be measured in seconds (s), minutes (min), or hours (h). Such an accelerometer would have numbers on it so the indicator could measure accelerations quantitatively in meters per second per second (m/s/s), miles per hour per second (mi/h/s), or any other units that indicate acceleration over some convenient range of values.

List of Suppliers

The following companies supply the materials that may be needed for science fair projects:

Carolina Biological Supply Co.
2700 York Road
Burlington, NC 27215
(800) 334-5551; http://www.carolina.com

Central Scientific Co. (CENCO)
3300 CENCO Parkway
Franklin Park, IL 60131
(800) 262-3626; http://www.cenconet.com

Connecticut Valley Biological Supply Co., Inc.
82 Valley Road, Box 326
Southampton, MA 01073
(800) 628-7748

Delta Education
P.O. Box 915
Hudson, NH 03051-0915
(800) 258-1302

Edmund Scientific Co.
101 East Gloucester Pike
Barrington, NJ 08007
(609) 547-3488

Fisher Science Education
485 S. Frontage Road
Burr Ridge, IL 60521
(800) 955-4663; http://www.fisheredu.com

Frey Scientific
100 Paragon Parkway
Mansfield, OH 44905
(800) 225-3739

Nasco-Modesto
P.O. Box 3837
Modesto, CA 95352-3837
(800) 558-9595; http://www.nasco.com

Nasco Science
P.O. Box 901
Fort Atkinson, WI 53538-0901
(800) 558-9595

Sargent-Welch/VWR Scientific
911 Commerce Court
Buffalo Grove, IL 60089-2375
(800) 727-4368; http://www.SargentWelch.com

Science Kit & Boreal Laboratories
777 East Park Drive
Tonawanda, NY 14150-6782
(800) 828-7777; http://sciencekit.com

Wards Natural Science Establishment, Inc.
5100 West Henrietta Road
P.O. Box 92912
Rochester, NY 14692-9012
(800) 962-2660; http://www.wardsci.com

Further Reading

Books

Barr, George. *Sports Science for Young People*. Mineola, N.Y.: Dover, 1990.

Cash, Terry. *101 Physics Tricks: Fun Experiments with Everyday Materials*. New York: Sterling, 1992.

Ehrlich, Robert. *The Cosmological Milkshake: A Semi-Serious Look at the Size of Things*. New Brunswick, N.J.: Rutgers University Press, 1995.

Gardner, Robert. *Experimenting with Light*. New York: Franklin Watts, 1991.

———. *Experimenting with Science in Sports*. New York: Franklin Watts, 1993.

———. *Famous Experiments You Can Do*. New York: Franklin Watts, 1990.

———. *Ideas for Science Projects*. New York: Franklin Watts, 1986.

———. *Investigating and Exploring Forces*. New York: Julian Messner, 1991.

———. *Investigating and Exploring Light*. New York: Julian Messner, 1991.

———. *More Ideas for Science Projects*. New York: Franklin Watts, 1989.

———. *Robert Gardner's Favorite Science Experiments*. New York: Franklin Watts, 1992.

———. *Science Projects About Light*. Springfield, N.J.: Enslow Publishers, Inc., 1994.

Goodwin, Peter. *Physics Projects for Young Scientists*. New York: Franklin Watts, 1991.

109

Hoyt, Marie A. *Kitchen Chemistry and Front Porch Physics*. New York: Educational Services Press, 1983.

Wood, Robert W. *Physics for Kids: Forty-Nine Easy Experiments in Electricity and Magnetism*. Blue Ridge Summit, Pa.: Tab Books, 1990.

Internet Addresses

Bloomfield, Louis A. *How Things Work*. n.d. <http://Landau1.phys. Virginia.EDU/Education/Teaching/HowThingsWork/> (November 16, 1999).

"The Exploratorium's Science of Cycling." n.d. <http://www. exploratorium.edu/cycling/> (November 16, 1999).

Henderson, Tom. "Glenbrook South Physics Home Page." August 13, 1998. <http://www.glenbrook.k12.il.us/gbssci/phys/phys. html> (November 16, 1999).

Lynds, Beverly T. "About Rainbows." September 19, 1995. <http:// www.unidata.ucar.edu/staff/blynds/rnbw.html> (November 16, 1999).

Pfaff, Raman. "Visualize Science!" *Explore Science*. n.d. <http:// www.explorescience.com> (November 16, 1999).

Index